THE
LOGOPHILE'S
ORGY

THE LOGOPHILE'S ORGY

Favorite Words of
Famous People

by
Lewis Burke Frumkes

Delacorte Press

Published by
Delacorte Press
Bantam Doubleday Dell Publishing Group, Inc.
1540 Broadway
New York, New York 10036

Library of Congress Cataloging in Publication Data

Frumkes, Lewis Burke.
    The logophile's orgy : favorite words of famous people /
by Lewis Burke Frumkes.
        p.   cm.
    ISBN 0-385-31352-7
    1. English language — Lexicology — Anecdotes.   2. Vo-
cabulary — Anecdotes.   I. Title.
PE1574.F73   1995
428.1 — dc20   94-19713
                                                   CIP

Manufactured in the United States of America
Published simultaneously in Canada

April 1995

10 9 8 7 6 5 4 3 2 1

BVG

For my students:
past, present, future.

Acknowledgments

In a project of this scope, help comes and is welcomed in many forms. Among those to whom I owe thanks:

Robin Rue, Robin Little, Richard Lederer, Karen Osborne, Wes Vause, Carol Bullard, Janice Bojac, Beth Wright, Cindy Atwood, Bob Harris, Alana Frumkes, Timothy Frumkes, Amber Frumkes, Roy Frumkes, Karen Kennerly, Tamara Moskowitz, Michael and Liz Yogman, Metthe de la Houssaye Dunk, Sidney Offit, Mark Cohen, Jeanne Cavelos, Arthur Indursky, Roz Drawers, Anita Berman, Juliet Gumbs, Flip Porter, Dudley Blodgett, Rosemarie Dackerman, Peter Green, Mimi Kazon, Peter Minichiello, Jackie Cantor, The New York Public Library, and of course to all the wonderful contributors, without whose words this book would not have been possible.

He liked words and images. "Blue" was one of his favorite words. He liked the feeling it made on his lips and tongue when he said it. Words have a physical feeling, not just meaning, he remembered thinking when he was young. He liked other words, such as "distant," "woodsmoke," "highway," "ancient," "passage," "voyageur," and "India" for how they sounded, how they tasted, and what they conjured up in his mind. He kept lists of words he liked posted in his room.

The Bridges of Madison County,
Robert James Waller

Summer afternoon—summer afternoon; to me those have always been the two most beautiful words in the English language.

Henry James

Author's Introduction

The Logophile's Orgy began as a wondering about other writers' favorite words, then grew into a project far beyond anything I had originally envisioned. Contributors one and all were unabashedly enthusiastic about complying with my query and often confessed to never having considered the question before. Through the responses sometimes one could discern the very landscape of a writer's mind, or his vision of life. When not being profound or revealing, writers were frequently witty or linguistically clever. Others were just direct and succinct.

The thrust of the book is that we all have favorite words, words that tickle our ears and please our eyes, words that we seem to use more often than other words. I, for example, use the words "eggplant" and "kumquat" more often in my writing than other words, though this may have more to do with the shape of the objects, ovoid, than with the sounds of the words . . .

I'm an egg man. Actually, if you noticed, I've used the word "more" more than "eggplant" or "kumquat" here, in fact more than I'd like in this one paragraph. Six times to be exact. If you pushed me farther, I'd tell you that "djinn" and "fey" and perhaps "seductive," "oneiric," and "enchantment" are favorite words as well because they are magical and mysterious, not to mention romantic.

And speaking of things mysterious and fey, no sooner had I penned "oneiric" into this introduction as one of my favorite words than what should appear in the mail in response to my query seeking favorite words but Dr. Wayne Myers's contribution to the book also citing "oneiric" as one of his favorite words and then Glenn Seaborg offering "kumquat." Days later, Judith Kelman wrote that "serendipity" was her favorite word, and Helen Handley too, and from Sri Lanka came Arthur C. Clarke's explanation of the origin of "serendipity"; it comes from his adopted country, Serendib, or Serendip, the ancient term for Ceylon. Like Leibnitz and Newton, who independently invented the calculus, Margaret Atwood and Fred Mustard Stewart both alighted on one of English's most obscure of words among their favorites, "chthonic" which means of or pertaining to the gods of the underworld.

Writers, for the most part, are more sensitive

to words than other people, because they use them all the time, and work with them, and sometimes bend them to their will. In fact, that is what got me doing this book in the first place — I had favorite words and I was curious what other writers' favorite words might be. Nor did it come as a surprise when several of the writers queried declared "onomatopoeia," a writer's word, to be their favorite word, or that Wes Craven, Wilfrid Sheed, and Sven Birkerts chose "plangent," the incessant and repeating sound of waves rolling up on the beach, as their selections. These are wonderful words, and writers are understandably attracted to them. Desmond Tutu, Anglican Bishop of Cape Town and a Nobel laureate for peace, as I recall, was enthralled by the word "wonderful" itself. Another group of contributors including columnist Ann Landers, publisher Al Goldstein, and cookbook writer Maida Heatter confessed to an outsized fondness for "chocolate" as a word and as a substance. "Callipygian," a word I first discovered as a youngster while reading an obscure Spanish writer in Spanish, surfaced as the favorite word of two contributors, Patrick McGrath and Robin Smith; and Tommy Boyle, aka T. Coraghessan Boyle, opted instead for "steatopygia."

Often writers literally love words, the way other people love children. They become almost possessive about them, which may account for why a few well-known writers insisted that they had no favorite words or at least were not willing to share them.

Nevertheless, I thought it would be useful and fun to see what many good writers, as well as scientists, educators, actors, and others who work with language, would find to be their favorite words. And the results were not only gratifying but on occasion actually astounding. In fact, as I mentioned earlier, what started as just a whimsical anthological work became an adventure so fascinating I couldn't wait to open the mail each day to see what the catch would bring. People poured their cleverness, their aesthetics, and often their hearts into their contributions, and you will enjoy these in just a moment.

Ray Bradbury selected "cinnamon," because "it causes me to think of voyages and ships on the sea and the Arabian Nights." John Updike responded with "anfractuous" and "phosphorescent" because that is how the world appears to him now that he is sixty. I wonder if any of us were John Updike, wouldn't we also see the world as aglow and phosphorescent? But Russell Baker, who in real life appears robustly happy and is certainly urbane, witty, and successful, curiously chose "melancholy" as one of his favorite words, and then added, "but if proper nouns may be considered, no word satisfies me more utterly than 'Pushtunistan.'" Larry King predictably and charmingly chose "why" as his word. Not only is it a word he uses professionally he says, but "it is the best word in the universe. Think about it."

Does genetics play a role in favorite words? Susan and Ben Cheever, sister and brother writers, independently and at different times sent me the words "yes" and "no" with contrasting reasons for their selections. John Kluge and Oscar de la Renta, who are not related, affirmed their fondness for the positive word "yes." However, Bel Kaufman preferred "no."

Abundantly forthcoming, as you would expect, were master wordsmiths Richard Lederer and Willard Espy, whose love of words was clearly reflected in their colorful selections of "usher" and "velleity." One linguistics mandarin (Noam Chomsky), on the other hand, when approached for a favorite word said he'd think about it but that he wasn't really good at this sort of thing, which caused Jack Driscoll to laugh and suggest that I write back, "If not you, who?"

Joyce Carol Oates showed a definite fondness for "palimpsest," Erica Jong, for "breath, and breathless," and Dave Barry, for "weasel." Leo Buscaglia, Joey Adams, and Rosanno Brazzi were all in love with "love," though each in his own special way. It got so that each day was an adventure in finding more wonderful words from other interesting and exciting people. Nobel laureates in physics Arno Penzias and Sheldon Glashow sent in their favorite words, Penzias providing a moving glimpse of his life under Hitler in 1938 in Germany, and Glashow demonstrating his impressive knowledge of languages by choosing words with interesting double and triple letters, "radii" and "skiing" and "hajji" in English and *Schneeeule* in German, and then pointing out that "indivisibility" has more *i*'s than any other English word he knows except its plural, which has seven. Henry Rosovsky, former dean of the School of Arts and Sciences at Harvard and the principal architect of the core curriculum, sent in the best definition of a liberal education that he had ever come across as his contribution to favorite words, and Willard V. O. Quine, one of this century's preeminent philosopher/logicians, wrote that Donald Davidson, another great philosopher, had told him he overdoes the word "actually" though he himself (Quine) is unaware of having any particular fondness for it.

Animals had their day. Margaret Drabble did a turn on "squirrels" and Pamela McCorduck on "frogs." And then more fabulous words arrived from Quentin Crisp and Cynthia Ozick; from Helen Gurley Brown, Dominick Dunne, Ed McMahon, Douglas Fairbanks, Jr., Gene Kelly and Gahan Wilson until my head began to swim from the delight of it all.

Patricia Volk, the author of *All It Takes*, said she was partial to *fuh-∂rayt, fuh-∂himmele∂, fuh-cocktuh, fuh-blon∂get,* and *fuh-tu∂hte∂,* five Yiddish words that mean crazy, mixed up, addled, lost, and wiped out. Just saying them, she says, and shrugging, makes you feel better. She also liked "euglena," as in the green protozoan with a single flagellum and a red pigment spot, and thereafter, to Pattie's amusement, I began to call her Euglena. "Euglena Volk," it has a certain ring, don't you think?

When it comes to choosing favorite words, there are many different approaches, but euphony is an apparently important and popular consideration. Language experts such as I. M. Pei, after examining some lists of most beautiful words from American and British writers in the forties, which included "dawn," "golden," "murmuring," and "lullaby," found that it was difficult to separate the words from their associations, and that perhaps the only objective way to measure the euphony of words would be to use judges who did not know the meanings of the words. In this regard, whether it originated with H. L. Mencken, who my friend Richard Lederer tells me once quoted a Chinese boy who was learning English as saying that "cellar door" contained the most musical combination of sounds he had ever heard in that language, or as Bill Cole suggests, that it was just the result of one of those lists that keep turning up, in this case, "The Most Beautiful Words in the English Language," which had as a winner—"cellar door," it is perhaps coincidental that four of the contributors to *The Logophile's Orgy* agreed by choosing "cellar door" as their favorite words as well.

Bruce Feirstein, who wrote *Real Men Don't Eat Quiche*, and who also loves the sounds of words, did not choose "quiche" but "flotilla" as his favorite word both for its special aural appeal and the appealing image it conjures up in his mind. Edgar Allan Poe more than many other poets understood how to make the sounds of words work for him and frequently employed "ore-sound" words such as "nevermore" and "lore" and "moor" to adumbrate (one of Ricardo Montalban's favorite words) the landscape of his poetry and convey a foreboding sense of gloom and forlornness. In case you hadn't noticed, persons writing love songs tend to employ *oo* words like "moon" and "croon" to create their special effects. "Moon over Miami, da, da, da, da, da, da . . ." And soon everybody is making goo-goo eyes and cooing and wooing.

Fashion also counts, and fashionable words such as "cobble" and "jerry-built" and "tad" tend to become favorite words among those in the know and intellectuals, while words such as "sufficient," "proleptic," "necessary," and "apodictic" find currency with philosophers and psychologists. Close your eyes now . . . okay, "shit," "fuck," and "schmuck" are also favorite words . . . and "you know" unquestionably led the pack as chief locutional weed of the insecure and the inarticulate . . . you know. Surprisingly and amusingly, two arch contributors to this book even wrote that "Frumkes" was their favorite word if names could be counted as words. And I accept that. What could be more flattering?

In short, this word project became a real labor of "love"—Joey Adams's, Rosanno Brazzi's, and Leo Buscaglia's favorite word (see above)—and I genuinely enjoyed the year and a half it took me to complete it. I came to understand what Phyllis Diller meant when she wrote "words are the playthings of the mind." Phyllis, besides being a gifted comic, pianist, and painter, also loves language, and loves to work and mold words as she would clay, and so do I.

It is my hope that perhaps reading what some of the world's most insightful writers, wittiest entertainers, leading educators, and most brilliant scientists have selected as their favorite words will inspire you to become more confident and creative when you use the language . . . will enlighten you and encourage you down new avenues of thought and imagination . . . will fascinate you . . . and at the very least amuse and entertain you.

Want to know what Norman Mailer's favorite words are? Read on!

LBF

Contributors

Floyd Abrams
Joey Adams
Hanan Al-Shaykh
John Ashbery
Margaret Atwood
Nicholson Baker
Russell Baker
Carole Baron
Dave Barry
Kenneth Battelle
Julie Baumgold
William Baumol
Orson Bean
Ira Berkow
Anne Bernays
Sven Birkerts
Bruce Bliven
Naomi Bliven
Antoinette Bosco
T. Coraghessan Boyle
Ray Bradbury
Rosanno Brazzi
Berke Breathed
Joe Bob Briggs

Helen Gurley Brown
Malcome Browne
Mario Buatta
Carol Bullard
Leo Buscaglia
Frank Carnabuci
Alan Caruba
Jeanne Cavelos
Ben Cheever
Susan Cheever
Ron Chernow
Mary Higgins Clark
Arthur C. Clarke
James Clavell
William Cole
Denton A. Cooley
Wes Craven
Quentin Crisp
Norm Crosby
Clive Cussler
Olivia de Havilland
Len Deighton
Oscar de la Renta
Edwin Diamond

Phyllis Diller

Rita Dove

Margaret Drabble

Jack Driscoll

Dominick Dunne

Andrea Dworkin

Paul Edwards

Albert Ellis

Willard Espy

Gloria Estefan

Douglas Fairbanks, Jr.

Barbara Silberdick
   Feinberg

Bruce Feirstein

Gary Fisketjon

Milos Forman

Richard Frances

Lewis Burke Frumkes

Melvin B. Frumkes

Roy Frumkes

Cristina Garcia

Howard Gardner

Murray Gell-Mann

Tom Gerety

Dick Gilbert

Penn Gillette

Nikki Giovanni

Sheldon Glashow

Harrison J. Goldin

Al Goldstein

Edward Gorey

Virginia Graham

Roger Granet

Alan "Ace" Greenberg

Dan Greenburg

A. R. Gurney, Jr.

Mark Hamill

Helen Handley

Don Hauptman

Jack Hausman

Naura Hayden

Maida Heatter

Florence Henderson

Tony Hendra

Bob Hope

A. E. Hotchner

Arianna Huffington

Derek Humphry

Evan Hunter

Susan Isaacs

Pico Iyer

Rona Jaffe

Dennis James

Morton Janklow

Tama Janowitz

Franklyn G. Jenifer

Richard Johnson

Erica Jong

Jenny Joseph

Bel Kaufman

Mimi Kazon

Edmund Keeley

Gene Kelly

Judith Kelman

Rose Kennedy

Victor Kiam

Florence King

Larry King

John Kluge

Joan Konner

Paul Krassner

Charles Krauthammer

Bernard Kripke

Hedy Lamarr

Felicia Lamport

Ann Landers

Lewis Lapham

Ring Lardner, Jr.

Eric Larsen

Robin Leach

David Leavitt

Guy Lebow

Richard Lederer

Richard Lefrak

Elmore Leonard

Charles Lindner

Art Linkletter

Gordon Lish

Phillip Lopate

Shirley Lord

Robert Ludlum

Roa Lynn

Yo-Yo Ma

Sirio Maccioni

Pamela McCorduck

Patrick McGrath

Ian MacKenzie

Ed McMahon

Norman Mailer

Robert Manning

Elaine Marks

Peter Martins

Bobbie Ann Mason

Dina Merrill

Ricardo Montalban

David Morrell

Desmond Morris

Frederic Morton

Jerome T. Murphy

Wayne Myers

Fae Myenne Ng

Joyce Carol Oates

Douglas O'Brien

Sidney Offit

Ben Okri

Frank Oz

Cynthia Ozick

Abraham Pais

Linus Pauling

David Pearce

David Pearson

Arno Penzias

Regina Peruggi

Steven Pinker

George Plimpton

Letty Cottin Pogrebin

Roman Polanski

Reynolds Price

W. V. Quine

Maxwell M. Rabb

Dan Rather

Lynn Redgrave

Leni Riefenstahl

Mandy Riner

Joan Rivers

A. M. Rosenthal

Jack Rosenthal

Henry Rosovsky

Wilbur Ross

Howard Rubenstein

Edward Said

Sabastiao Salgado

Harrison Salisbury

Abbie Salny

Stephen Sandy

Francesco Scavullo

George Schindler

Mary Schmidt-
    Campbell

Steven Schragis

Robert Schuller

Glenn Seaborg

Wilfrid Sheed

Cybill Shepherd

Jane Smiley

Robin Smith

Albert Solnit
Stephen Spahn
Gloria Steinem
Robert J. Sternberg
Fred Mustard Stewart
Leo Stone
Mark Strand
Whitley Strieber
Gay Talese
Maria Tallchief
Amy Tan
Lionel Tiger
Barbara Tober
Diana Townsend-
   Butterworth
Joseph F. Traub

Laurence Tribe
Desmond M. Tutu
John Updike
Sander Vanocur
Gwen Verdon
Patricia Volk
Tom Wallace
Wendy Wasserstein
Nancy Willard
Edward O. Wilson
Gahan Wilson
Hilma Wolitzer
Stephen Wright
Michael Yogman
William Zinsser
Elmo R. Zumwalt, Jr.

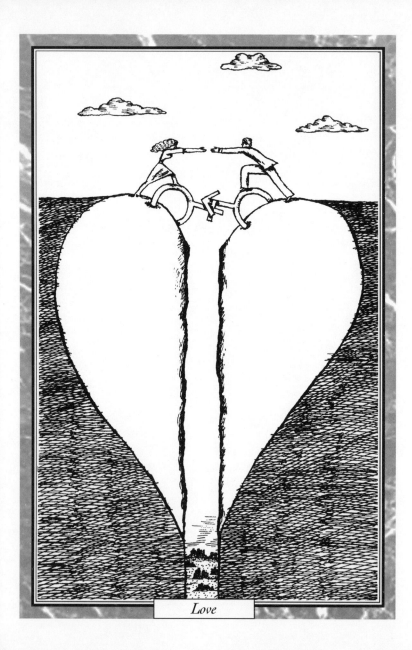

Love

Floyd Abrams

*(New York attorney, partner, Cahill,
Gordon & Reindell)*

My favorite word is "iguana."

Joey Adams

(Comedian, columnist)

My favorite word in the world is "love." I was
born with it, I grew up with it, and I live by it.

I was marching with Martin Luther King to
prove the integration law which was named after
me in show business because I said I didn't believe in Black singers or Jewish dancers or
Spanish musicians. They were simply either
singers or dancers or musicians. We were marching down Fifth Avenue, and people were throw-
ing eggs at us along with obscenities about
Blacks and Jews. As we marched arm in arm, I
asked, "Reverend, how do you handle your ene-
mies?" He said, *"Love* the hell out of them." And
that's what I've done all my life.

When I was a young man, President John F.
Kennedy sent me around the world as the Goodwill Ambassador. My first stop was in Vietnam,
in 1961. The world was in utter turmoil. JFK

1

said, as I was leaving for my job of peace, "Use a joke instead of a stick. Use love instead of a bomb."

In forty years of the most beautiful marriage, there has never been one unhappy moment in my life, and it's all because of one word: "love."

●◆ ●◆ ●◆

Hanan Al-Shaykh
(Author, The Story of Zahra)

Washwasha. It means "a whisper" in Arabic, and it sounds exactly like a whisper.

"Reminiscent." Whenever I hear it, I visualize two delicate hands trying to pick up things. Maybe this image has to do with the word *rammasser* in French.

"Frangipani." Whenever I hear it, I smell my childhood. In Beirut, my neighborhood was full of frangipani trees.

"Err." Like an animal sound.

"Fascination." It was my first English word I like to remember after it was repeated over and over in the film *Love in the Afternoon* since Audrey Hepburn was my idol only because she gave me confidence; to be slim is all right and even complimentary in a society which considers it a drawback. After seeing the film, I kept asking what does the word "fascination" mean, to no avail, until I became seventeen years old. I thought I was superior; I could speak English; I could say "fantastic," "fantasy," "fantasia," and "fascination."

John Ashbery
(Poet, Flow Chart; Self-portrait
in a Convex Mirror)

My favorite words are "climate," "meretricious," and "intermittent." I wonder what it all means . . .

Margaret Atwood
(Author, The Handmaiden's Tale; Cat's Eye;
The Robber Bride)

Here are my words:
Thirty years ago, my favorite words were "chthonic" and "igneous." (I was in my Pre-Cambrian Shield phase.) Then they became "jungoid," "musilagenous," and "larval" (biology took over). Right now they are "diaphanous" and "lunar." The latter especially, as it combines rock

and light, solidity and inaccessibility, with a suggestion of tidal activity, and howling wolves.

Nicholson Baker

(Author, U & I: A True Story; Vox*)*

Of abstract nouns containing the letter *l*, my favorites are "reluctance" and "revulsion."

The "luct" in "reluctance" functions as an oral brake or clutch ("clutch" and "luct" being sonic kin), making the word seem politely hesitant, tactful, circumspect—willing to let the hired tongue have its fun before completing its meaning.

My uncle tried to teach me how to say "revulsion" properly when I was five: under his tutelage the second syllable became a kind of Shakespearean dry heave. The word is full of exuberant, *l*-raising relish and revelry.

The first word I liked was "broom."

Russell Baker

(Columnist, The New York Times)

"Melancholy" is one of my favorite words, but if proper nouns may be considered, no word satisfies me more utterly than "Pushtunistan." Can you bear a fardel? The funniest word in English is "fardel," the most pompous is "obloquy," the most unnecessary is "congeries," and the hardest to pronounce without sounding like a twit is "prescient."

Carole Baron

(President and publisher, Dell Publishing)

"Obfuscate." A useful word to use when politeness is required and when someone is clearly and deliberately obscuring information or holding back for his/her own agenda.

Dave Barry

(Syndicated columnist, humorist)

I am very partial to "weasel." It's hard to imagine a thought that wouldn't be improved by the addition of a "weasel." For example:

Weak: "Spiro Agnew was vice president from 1969 through 1973."

Better: "Spiro Agnew was vice president from 1969 through 1973. What a weasel."

Another excellent word is *qua* because most people (me, for example) have no idea what it means. So *qua* tends to lend an air of unchallengeable authority to a statement.

Weak: "The Mets suck."

Better: "The Mets *qua* Mets suck."

And of course you can't go wrong with "sputum."

Kenneth Battelle

(World-renowned hairdresser,
Kenneth of Kenneth's Salon)

I think the three-letter words that end in *ex*—i.e., "hex," "Mex," "rex," "sex," "Tex," "vex"—are amazing, as they conjure so much of a sense of power and are so descriptive.

I love "curmudgeon," as I would like to be one. Maybe I am. And I love "dichotomy," as I find the world to be just one big one.

Julie Baumgold

(Contributing editor, Esquire *magazine; author,*
Creatures of Habit)

"Night," because the night forgives, it keeps secrets, cloaks the bad things of the day, hides ugliness, because you feel you can pass through it invisibly, because the people of the night see more in the shield of darkness. Almost any word sounds better to me with "night" in front of or behind it and the best word of all is "tonight." As Dracula said, "Listen to them—the children of the night. What sweet music they make."

William Baumol

(Economist, director, C.V. Starr Center for Applied Economics, NYU)

My favorite words are "chutzpah," "ambiguity," and "chimera." The word "chutzpah," which can't even be spelled properly, much less translated fully, from the Yiddish is perhaps primus inter pares among the trove of Yiddish words rich in nuance and content. Meaning a compound of audacity and sheer gall, all carried out with panache, competence, and a touch of humor, there seems to be no substitute in any other language.

"Ambiguity" is one of my favorites because I consider it to be the crucial attribute of any work of art that has any prospect of enduring. Good examples are the Bach cantatas, which, after all, were prepared as pieces of Lutheran propaganda. If their content were unambiguous, would they still attract the many Oriental musicians who perform them so superbly, and to whom their Lutheran origins can mean very little?

"Chimera" recommends itself to me because I just like the sound and like the concept. Does it need more justification than that?

Orson Bean

(Actor, Dr. Quinn,
Medicine Woman; *humorist, author)*

"Belly button" is the word.

I love it because it makes me laugh and because it collects belly button "lint," for which
there is no known use. We need more totally useless things in life.

Ira Berkow

(Sports columnist, The New York Times)

My offering for favorite word is "bamboozle."
The sound of the word gives instant delight, and
brings a smile to one's face, unless of course you
yourself have been bamboozled, or the target of a
bamboozle—that is, tricked, cheated, or conned.
I looked up the derivation and the dictionary
says "obscure origins," which adds to the joy. It
obviously was invented because we needed such
a juicy word. The happy placing of the pair of *b*'s,
the twin *o*'s, the earthy *m*, the lurking *l*, and the
zippy *z* provide a word of nonpareil pronunciation. You can say it with the long *boo*—"bam-
boooozle"—or with a kind of Yiddish accent, giving the *oo*'s a softer, tighter, bosomy sound.

To be sure, there are numerous words in our rich mother tongue that are a pleasure to let roll from our lips. But when asked to select my favorite word, it was "bamboozle" that first popped into mind. Why, I don't know. I rarely use the word, so it must simply have been lying in wait in my subconscious to spring up at this very moment. And since I believe it is usually sound advice to stick to initial instincts, I do so now with this luscious and loony word.

Anne Bernays
(Author, Professor Romeo)

Nice of you to ask me about my favorite words. Here they are, four of them.

"Eighty-seven." In my family this is a generic number meaning "many." As in "When I went to get my driver's license renewed, there were eighty-seven people waiting in line in front of me." Or "This is the eighty-seventh time this week I've asked you to clean up the mess in your room." Justin claims that it probably derives from Lincoln's Gettysburg Address—"Fourscore and seven years ago . . ."—but I'm doubtful. In any case, eighty-seven is an all-purpose number, making a clear statement. It's very useful.

My other three words—"fat," "old," "conceited"—belong together and are examples of the kind of straight language I admire and mourn the loss of. All are routinely euphemized, as in "obese," "overweight," "husky," "aging," "elderly," and some form of (yuck) "senior citizen," "narcissistic," "entitled," "self-absorbed." Why can't we call things by their true names?

Sven Birkerts

(Essayist, author, American Energies: Essays on Fiction)

Favorite words . . . I've been going about for days now tilting my head and blinking as the candidates have it out in the cranial arena, and I've decided that it's too hard to choose from an unlimited field. Why not just stab the dictionary with a knife like the Dadaists did? But no, the better solution is to impose a constraint. Mine? I will select, somewhat at random, a small crop of beauts from Malcolm Lowry's *Under the Volcano*. Because this novel, about the last day in the life of Geoffrey Firmin—drunkard, Consul—once intoxicated me as no cruder distillation has ever managed. I'm not sure I could ever explain the process, the chemical transaction, but I will say that Lowry, even more than Joyce or Woolf, infected me with his obvious love for distinct words—for their look, their sound, their suggestiveness, as well as for the way they jostle together in a line of print, seducing the eye-beam, playing crack-the-whip down in the recesses of the ear. An homage, then, a *sortes Lowriae:*

plangent, sculpturings, lacquered, naphtha, waxplants, spoliation, mescal, thaumaturgy, coquelicot, casuistry, strychnine, whiskerando, Pleiades, anis, jai-alai, abbatoir, plantains, dolorous, bougainvillea, chamois, thrumming, horripilating, multitudinously, exacerbated, cobalt, hippodrome, rajah, toothmug, antipodes, gesticulations, barranca, parapet, mirador, runcible, monarchical, immedicable, pariah, convulvulus, pyramidal, cashiered, dementia, pulque, sulfurously, bedraggedly, honeymoon, calvados, digestif, mestizo, Palladium, mosque, bobolink, jocosely, confetti, assuaged, orchestras, elastic, borracho, confederate, pocketing, ventilated, pandemonium.

Bruce Bliven

(Editor and writer, The New Yorker)

By far my favorite word is "cat." I know how to spell it. As the product of what was known as a "progressive school" in the 1920s, I can spell only a handful of words with equal assurance. And in addition, I have enjoyed a personal relationship with at least one cat, and more often two cats, almost all of my life. I have learned, as a result, that two cats are easier than one because some of the outrageous demands a cat makes are directed to the other cat rather than to his or her person. I've liked the cats I've known well, and I wish I'd had the chance to know some of their family *(Felidae)* members better, especially lions, tigers, leopards, jaguars, cougars, wildcats, lynx, and cheetahs. And next to "cat" as a noun, perhaps my second favorite is "cat" as a prefix. I like catfish, catsup, and catalogs, although I am not especially fond of caterpillars. Above all—this paragraph reminds me—I am categorically devoted to catnaps.

Naomi Bliven

(Book reviewer, The New Yorker)

Though there are many things (chocolate, for instance) that I like very much, the words for my favorite things aren't favorite words. In fact, I think I dislike favorite words—especially other people's favorite words. Remember the years when every writer accused everybody else of "hubris"? And when reviewers called every okay performance an epiphany? Years ago I tried to float a comparatively unfamiliar word, "vatic," to see how far it would go, but my editor immediately changed it to "prophetic." After "irenic" was changed to "ironic," I decided to accept the limitations of other people's vocabularies. My favorite words are words everybody knows.

Antoinette Bosco

(Executive editor, Litchfield County Times;
author, Marriage Encounter;
The Pummeled Heart)

The word first rolled from my mother's lips when I was maybe five or six. She was telling me a story, about a man, who wore "pantaloons." She had a way of stretching out the last sound so that I couldn't let go of its ring in my ears. "Pantaloon," I would say, for no reason at all, on a regular basis until I got old enough to embarrass myself.

Then one day I happened to come upon a colorful bit of information about my favorite word. It seems that there was a very holy man in Venice who wore baggy pants. He is remembered as Saint Pantaleone, but the style in pants that he set is remembered more than he is. My favorite word had history and tradition. Made me feel good.

"Pumpernickel" had a sound that made me smile, with a taste that made me frown. What fun it was to discover that this word, too, had a history, said to have come from a remark that Napoleon made when he first tasted it—*"pain pour Nicol"*—that being his horse!

Then there are words that seduce me simply because they make me feel, or react, to their syllables—such as crystal, awesome, jewel, jingle, flamingo, zenith, buckle, ginger.

And I mustn't leave out "honeymoon." Clearly this was chosen to express a belief that marriage is sweetest right after the ceremony—the "honey" time. But where did the "moon" part come in? Dr. Samuel Johnson, who long ago wrote the *Dictionary of the English Language,* figured out the answer (and I never doubt him, since he and I share the same birthday, September 18!). He figured the honey lasted about a month and that no sooner was the moon full than the sweetness would begin to wane. No matter. "Honeymoon" remains high among my favorite words.

T. Coraghessan Boyle
(Author, East Is East; World's End)

My favorite word (of the moment, anyway) is "steatopygia," which refers to "excessive fatness of the hips and buttocks, especially as found among the Hottentots and certain other African tribes, particularly among the women" *(Webster's New Twentieth Century Dictionary,* unabridged, second edition). I first came across the term during my research for *Water Music,* and I liked the idea of this evolutionary holdover—the fat so stored could be drawn upon by the depleted system in times of drought and duress. (A certain Seattle rapper has made his reputation on a song testifying to the usefulness and beauty of this adaptation, by the way.) For me, of course, the term has special significance too, beyond its use in my African novel and its splendid display in the flesh on our streets today, as I myself have inherited very little in the way of additional flesh from my ancestors. In fact, my own buttocks can be said to be entirely "nugatory."

Ray Bradbury

(Science fiction author, The Martian Chronicles; Dandelion Wine)

My two words are "ramshackle" and "cinnamon."

It's hard to explain why "ramshackle" has played such a part in my writing. I've found myself using it in essays and stories to describe certain situations which, I suppose, are part of all of our lives. Half the time we feel we are ramshackle people, lopsided, no right or left side of the brain, with some terrible vacuum in between. That, to me, is ramshackle. The way we lead our lives; my life is a litter of junk around my office, which has driven my wife and children mad. If anyone is ramshackle, it is yours truly.

The word "cinnamon" derives, I suppose, from visiting my grandma's pantry when I was a kid. I loved to read the labels on the spice boxes; curries from far places in India and cinnamons from across the world. The word causes me to think of voyages and ships on the sea and the Arabian Nights. I've used it in books such as *The Martian Chronicles* and many other stories. I find that over the years, I have to go back and take it out of stories because I've used it too often. One of the last times was in describing a wild Hollywood character, Constance Rattigan, in my novel *A Graveyard for Lunatics,* in which I describe her basic color as cinnamon. I don't seem to be able to give up on the word.

Rosanno Brazzi

(Actor, South Pacific; The Barefoot Contessa)

How could I say I "love" if I did not know the "word."

18

Berke Breathed

(Syndicated cartoonist, Bloom County; Outland)

Favorite real words:
   "butt," "higgledy-piggledy," "nincompoop," "bosom."
   Favorite fake, meaningless word:
   "renoberated."
   To be used when one simply can't think of the correct one.

Joe Bob Briggs

(Humorist, author, A Guide to Western Civilization, or My Story)

The most beautiful word I ever heard is *estacionamiento.* It's Spanish. After I learned to say it elegantly, musically, I found out what it means: parking lot.

Helen Gurley Brown

(Founder and editor, Cosmopolitan)

My favorite words are "comprehensive," "unilateral," "reciprocity." I don't know why I use them so much—I don't even *like* them. There are so many more beautiful words such as "rhapsody," "exquisite," "indigenous," and "tranquil," but I never *use* them. Using the favorite threesome must make me feel important or something.

Malcome Browne

(Science writer, The New York Times)

My word: "scarlet." It has a pleasant sound, rhymes with "starlet," suggests pleasurable sin, and is synonymous with bright red . . . my favorite color.

Reciprocity

21

Mario Buatta

(Fabulous decorator-designer)

I don't know about a favorite word, but I was accused by a *former* assistant of using the word "fabulous" too often. So often one morning that he counted twenty-two "fabulous"'s by 11 A.M.! That's eleven an hour!

I guess for a decorator/designer it's par-usual, but I never even listen to myself—much less go near a mirror *to get the visual image*!!! So I guess "fabulous" is it.

Thanks for including me among such a fabulous group. I think the idea of favorite words in book form is pretty fabulous, and if I were a real Italian, it would be *fabuloso*!

All best—and to Mrs. F.

Fabulously yours (too grandiose here!),

Mario

December 10, 1992—The Fabulous Stormy Day!

Carol Bullard

(Former Director of Development, Yaddo)

Though no writer of note (indeed no writer at all!), let me add one word which comes to my mind, which is "eleemosynary." To be sure, as one who labors in the philanthropic vineyard, it is a natural, but I really do think it is quite a special word, both in the way it rolls off the tongue and in its spelling, which is probably why Lee Blessing chose it as the title of one of his recent plays.

Leo Buscaglia

(Psychologist, author, Living, Loving & Learning)

What a delightful idea . . . a book of favorite words! Everyone who works/plays with words each day has such a list. Words that choke, that soothe, that frustrate, that delight, that stimulate.

As for those that tickle my ear, may I start with "love," "rapture," "ecstasy" (which also tickle my heart), and "frump," "quagmire," "phlegm," "loquacious," and "malleable," which sound and look delightfully goofy to me, and tickle my fancy.

Thanks for including me in the fun.

Panoply

Frank Carnabuci

(Headmaster, The Birch Wathen-Lenox School, New York)

My favorite word is "uncommon" (e.g., "She is a student of uncommon ability"). I enjoy this word greatly because it quickly sets someone or something apart from the larger masses. At the same time, "uncommon" invites further inquiry to establish why the person or object stands out.

Alan Caruba

(Writer and creator of one of the nation's most popular media spoofs, The Boring Institute)

The use of the word "panoply" will instantly accord you the status of an extremely well-educated, worldly-wise sophisticate. At least, I think it does. I have no idea why "panoply" holds such a fascination for me, but as a professional writer, I have conspired for years to find ways to sneak it into the text of anything I happen to be writing at the time. Technically, "panoply" means a complete array of a warrior's armor and weapons; a protective covering; or an impressive display. I tend to use the third definition since I rarely, if ever, have written about a warrior's armor and weapons. "Panoply" is one of those words you pick up in college and then try to slip into conversations to impress others, only to discover they have no idea what you're saying. In crowded parties, people tend to think I'm saying, "I'm planning to plea," and leave swiftly, believing I've recently been indicted for some crime. However, in print, "panoply" impresses the daylights out of editors who, of course, must look it up in their dictionary. It adds a lot of class to an otherwise pedestrian treatise on the mating habits of *Blattella germanica* (cockroaches to you, fella!). Hey! It's a living, okay?

Jeanne Cavelos

(Former senior editor, Dell Publishing)

I've had different favorite words at different times in my life. When I was little, I delighted in saying "doy" or "chunk of dough." Those words still make me laugh.

These days, I have two favorites. I love the word "faux." I first really learned to appreciate this word watching the home shopping channels, which addicted me for many months. In their glamorous parlance, vinyl became faux leather and cut glass became faux diamonds. The word itself is deceptive; it doesn't look the way it sounds. And when you insert it before a noun, that noun ends up taking on the exact opposite meaning.

My other favorite word is "irritant." Captain Kirk of *Star Trek* brought this word to my attention when he called someone an irritant. There are so many irritants in our lives—long lines at the grocery store, television news anchors, telephone salespeople—and sometimes I get very aggravated. But if I can just say (or scream), "This is an irritant!" it makes me feel better. The feel of the word in my mouth, the sound of it, brings me joy. And then everything's okay.

Go figure!

Ben Cheever

(Author, The Plagiarist)

At first I thought my favorite word was "adroit." Because of the way it sounds, and because I'm not.

But then I remembered that when my first son first went to school, he came back with two new words. These were "no" and "mine."

Both good, but if I had to choose a single syllable, above all others, it would have to be "yes."

27

I know it doesn't sound like much. Or rather it sounds like something a snake might do. But meaning's got to count for something. Besides, it's simple, elegant, and so rarely heard.

Susan Cheever
(Author, Looking for Work; A Woman's Life)

My favorite words are "yes" and "no." They are the us-words, the words that say it all. I love them for their completeness, their simplicity, and their appropriateness to all occasions. Are they not, after all, the most powerful words we have? Yes?

Ron Chernow
(Prize-winning biographer,
The House of Morgan, The Warburgs)

To the unsuspecting reader, the writer's life seems a monkish and solitary one, a drily monotonous grind. Every writer has encountered the cocktail party platitude, "You must be *very* disciplined." "On the contrary," I always reply, "I am completely out of control. If you must know, I have far more trouble stopping than starting."

We writers are closet hedonists, luxuriating in a wilderness of words. Words shower down upon us like manna, gratifying the senses as much by what our imaginations impart as by the secret flavors they contain. I confess a partiality to words that titillate several senses at once—juicy, rounded, succulent words that swell in the mouth and burst like overripe fruit. Words that vibrate with color, beauty, and intensity, expressing the plenitude of life: brilliant, vivid, exquisite, luscious, gorgeous, and voluptuous. Certain clusters of words seem to fascinate me: engaging, enchanting, enthralling; shine, sheen, shimmer, shadow; bewitching, bedizened, bedazzled. I fervently await the day that opalescent or adamantine will suddenly arise as *le mot juste* in a paragraph. Since cheating is forbidden upon pain of expulsion from the craft, I may have to wait decades just to unsheathe these two fancy words.

In short, nobody should pity writers their spare, ascetic lives. For while the world goes about its more serious work, we sit hunched over our word processors, far from view, reveling in our own secret world of musical sounds. Bet you didn't expect to hear this, Frumkes, from a so-called business historian?

Mary Higgins Clark

(Bestselling author; Remember Me;
Loves Music, Loves to Dance)

My favorite word is "memories." It always brings back the glad and sad of all the yesterdays, the salad days, the solemn and hilarious days, the bitter and the sweet days, the hectic and the neat days. "Memories," the word. That is the DNA of a writer!

Arthur C. Clarke

(Science fiction writer; 2001: A Space Odyssey)

"Incarnadine" (from *Macbeth)* is one of my favorites, but I seldom have a chance to use it!

So I'll settle for "Serendib" or "Serendip" and its derivatives—because I live here! I've even used it in a book title: *The View from Serendip.*

Serendip (or Serendib) is one of the many ancient names of Ceylon; it derives from the Muslim traders' Sarandib. The Greeks and Romans called the island Taprobane; the indigenous name was Sri Lanka ("the Resplendent Land"), and since 1972 this has been its official designation, though the national airline is still Air Ceylon, and no one ever talks of Sri Lanka tea.

From *The View from Serendip* (Random House)

Memories

James Clavell

(Author; Shōgun; Noble House)

My favorite words . . .
  "Once upon a time . . ."

William Cole

(Writer of light verse)

I go for "alabaster"—goes trippingly off the tongue. The same for "lapis lazuli"—as pretty as it sounds. The star "Aldeberan" sounds like a lovely, faraway star. And "turnpike" is good—especially its abbreviation—"tpke," which I pronounce tup-key. And there's nothing wrong with "cunt"! Sounds like it can be only one thing. And a fine thing it is! And "caboose" sounds like a jolly little red car bouncing along at the end of a train. (No more, alas!) I enclose a few pages from an autobiography of mine relating to what is often quoted—along with Henry James's "summer afternoon"—"cellar door."

When my then wife was about to have the other child, we spent a long time thumbing through lists of names, noting down possibilities. At one point I had some sport with her. One of those lists that keep turning up—"The Most Beautiful Words in the English Language"—had, as a winner, "cellar door." Lovely sound to it. So I casually said one evening, "How about Selador? Isn't that pretty?" She said, "Ummm, nice. Where's it from?" "Oh . . . the Persian, the ancient Persian," I quickly fabricated. But suppose it's a girl? she asked. "Oh, then," I said, "we use the female version, 'Celador.' "

Denton A. Cooley

(Cardiac surgeon)

The word "eleemosynary" is one which I find useful when referring to charitable purposes. I find the word "paradigm" also useful.

Frequently I refer to success vs. failure and victory vs. defeat.

Wes Craven

(Film writer/director,
A Nightmare on Elm Street)

Here's my answer, three months later, to your query about my favorite word. Sorry for the delay, but three trips to Europe, four scripts, and a TV pilot kinda got in the way.

All of which should lead up to my favorite word being "procrastinate," although it's actually one of my *least* favorite words—probably because I've always felt it described so many of my actions so terribly well.

Anyway, my favorite word? "Plangent." I just think it's such a wonderfully evocative and elegant word. In second place I'd have to put "squinch," which is a sort of corbeling, but every time I use it, people think I'm making it up!

Quentin Crisp

(Author, The Naked Civil Servant)

I make every effort *not* to have a favorite word. I find that, if I write carelessly, I later have to delete the word "extraordinary" several times from each page, which must mean that I use it often in my heart but I couldn't say that it—or any—particular word is a "favorite." I'm not sure that I know what the word means. Isn't it a sin to have a favorite word?

Mr. Graves said:

Words repeated over and over
till the sense sickens in them and all but dies—
these The Great Devil, tenderly as a lover,
will lay his hand upon and hypnotise.

Norm Crosby
(Comedian)

My word is "apocryphal," and it comes from a nursery rhyme:

"Sing a song of sixpence apocryphal of rye," etc.

Also I like: "acrylic"—someone who reviews shows!

"Romance"—like, if you had a picnic in a Roman park, you'd probably find . . .

"Sacrament"—the capital of California—and "cabaret"—a hat worn by a French taxi driver!

Clive Cussler
(Author, Raise the *Titanic;* Inca Gold)

I love to end a chapter by making something or someone disappear "as though they never existed."

Then the trick is, where in hell do you go from there??

Olivia de Havilland
(Actress, The Snake Pit; The Heiress)

I understand your preoccupation with words and am charmed by the various examples which your letter cited. I am myself attracted by almost any French word—written or spoken: all those *aux, eux,* and *eaux* are so beautiful to read and so lovely to hear. Before I knew its meaning, I thought *saucisson* so exquisite that it seemed the perfect name to give a child—until I learned it meant sausage!

Len Deighton

(Mystery writer; The Ipcress File;
Catch a Falling Spy)

"Grace."

Not only does it sound as smooth as silk, but
the word's meanings extend from attractive (appearance), through willingness and musical frol-
ics and special on-campus terms, to its use as an
aristocratic title. And it has special religious significance too. Don't listen to me—look it up in a
big dictionary. It's a fine word.

Grace

Oscar de la Renta
(Fashion designer)

My favorite word is "yes," because I'm a positive person.

Edwin Diamond
(Media columnist, New York *magazine; author,*
Behind the Times)

I read somewhere that "cellar door" and "summer afternoon" were the nicest-sounding words in the English language. I also like neologisms; for instance, I claimed "newzak" (for TV news) as my own, but someone else was there first (Malcolm Muggeridge).

So I vote for "memory lane" (a stroll down). It resonates with a bygone America and seems a model for how the brain works physically.

Phyllis Diller

(Comic, entertainer, TV personality)

I love words like "aurora borealis." I see pastel colors in my mind's eye when I think of that word. I adore words like "ephemeral," "melifluous," "diaphanous," "glissando," "whispering," and "shimmering." These are a few of my favorite words. They ripple forward softly, suggesting music and beauty.

In my work as a stand-up comic, I must use monosyllabic words, ugly shock words. The operative joke word must end the gag and hopefully be a one-syllable word ending with an explosive consonant as in "butt."

"Agamemnon," "Beelzebub," "lollipop," and "Mississippi" are funny words.

"Plague," "torture," and "bomb" are terrifying words.

"Antidisestablishmentarianism" is a long word.

"Sweet, precious, darling" are loving words.

Words are wonderful. They are the playthings of the mind.

Rita Dove

(Pulitzer Prize–winning poet and novelist,
Through the Ivory Gate)

A favorite word from my childhood is "ragamuffin." Oh, how I loved the shaggy-dog compactness of this word. It applied to my favorite afterschool program, *The Little Rascals,* ragamuffins every one (except the boringly cute Darla); and I thought of it every time we had corn muffins for Sunday breakfast, warm and golden and crumbly. Whenever my parents used the word "ragamuffin" to instill shame in me, I smiled secretly and felt vindicated, inviolate in my essential child-ness.

A more adult preference came with university life and an understanding of irony at its bone-deepest level—that is, the irony between the sound of a word and its meaning. For me, "barbiturate" exemplified this dichotomy: what a delicious, seductive word, beautiful and inviting with its softened *t*'s and shooshy, shifting center. How ironic, then, that our culture has reduced its thrust to a convenient pharmaceutical!

Margaret Drabble
(Author, The Realms of Gold)

On this occasion I will select as my favorite word "squirrel." This is partly because I like the elegant little creature itself, and have a fondness for words with the somewhat neglected letter *q* in them. Also, I myself have a slight difficulty in pronouncing the letter *r;* but my husband rolls an *r* beautifully, and I try to encourage him to speak of squirrels whenever an opportunity arises. This is quite often as he, too, is fond of them and can easily be enticed to speak of them. We have them in the garden and we can hear them playing noisily on the bedroom roof. These are gray squirrels, not the almost-vanished native British red ones, but we like gray ones, too, and deplore the habit of redescribing them as tree rats in order to discourage affection for them.

The very fact that one can arouse hostility to a squirrel by calling it a rat shows the power of the Word. It is a small but significant illustration of how we can manipulate or be manipulated by language. Why should we feel free to poison a rat but not a squirrel?

Perhaps I should say a word, too, in favor of Beatrix Potter's fine story *Squirrel Nutkin,* in my view her masterpiece. I look forward to reading this to my grandchildren.

Jack Driscoll

*(Professor of mathematics,
Marymont Manhattan College)*

My favorite word is "syzygy," because it sounds
so nice, has a highly technical yet understandable
meaning both in astronomy and in prosody, and
especially because when written in script it has a
wonderful concatenation of loops.

I also like "adjective," because it's a noun, and
"butterfly," since it "flutters by" and translates
into *papillon* (French), *mariposa* (Spanish), *far-
falla,* (Italian), and *Schmetterling* (German).

Dominick Dunne

(Author, The Two Mrs. Grenvilles; An
Inconvenient Woman)

As a born people watcher, I have always been
drawn to the word "riveted" when applied to
people's behavior. "I was riveted." It could mean
that I was either fascinated or appalled by the
behavior, but more important, it means that I
was utterly absorbed in the viewing of it.

I also like the word "swell," either as an adjective or a noun. In my youth, it was slang,
frowned upon by teachers. But now, in its adjective usage, it is to me a perfect word to describe
approval of someone or something. As a noun, I
like to use it to describe an upper-class person of
impeccable lineage and style. There is still a
hangover of slang about it, which appeals to me.

In my latest novel, *A Season in Purgatory,* I
searched and searched for a word to describe an
emotional feeling that one character has for another. It was not love. It was not obsession. It
was more than fascination. Finally, I hit upon the
word "transfixed." It was perfect for my purposes. I have grown deeply attached to it. My
Chapter One ends with these sentences:

> Transfixed. What an odd word. Was I trans-
> fixed with Constant Bradley? Yes I was. I was
> completely transfixed by Constant Bradley.

Andrea Dworkin

(Author, feminist)

I like the word "autumn," probably because I like the season, but also because I like the silent *n*.

I like the words "lambent" and "poignant" although I never use them.

I particularly like the words "earth," "wind," "dust," "ash," "dark," "sad," and I use them often.

Paul Edwards

(Philosopher, editor,
The Encyclopedia of Philosophy)

Here are some of my favorite words. I have been collecting them during the last few weeks. It is quite a long list and at the end I will try to explain what I like about them:

bamboozle, pulverize, flamboyance, irretrievable, unflappable, unpalatable, rambunctious, gibberish, modulate, promulgate, convoluted (as in convoluted style), unadulterated balderdash, hodgepodge, mishmash, pussyfoot, gobbledygook, flipflop, bosh, maliferous, bombinate, sonorous, resound, voluptuous, fragrant, vitriolic, gerrymander

I think that what pleases me about these words is primarily their "music." In some cases the meaning is already suggested by the way the word sounds; in others it is not, but even so they are not dull or flat. Even a person who speaks in a very colorless tone cannot help getting some pleasing sound out of these words. You may of course have additional explanations which do not occur to me at the moment. This is an elusive business.

Albert Ellis

(Clinical psychologist, author, educator)

Meshugge—crazy, mixed up, addled. I love this word because it aptly describes practically all of my psychotherapy clients, because most of them nicely accept this description, and because they particularly accept it as being highly descriptive of their parents, close relatives, and intimate friends. Saying someone is crazy is often offensive; describing them as *meshugge* rarely is.

Willard Espy

*(Author of a dozen books
on language and language play)*

My favorite word! You can't miss; I expect to find in it some of the most irresistible essays since Ivor Brown's. I doubt, though, whether I can be of much use, partly because of my utter lack of energy these days and partly because any word I may happen to utter or write at any instant is for that instant my favorite of them all, the best thing that ever happened—until the following word shoulders it aside. Words are *all* my favorites, like women.

If you had said the most beautiful word, or the ugliest word, the job would have been a little simpler. A few years ago I made an arbitrary choice of the ten most beautiful words in English for *The Book of Lists,* and they have recently asked me to provide them with the ten ugliest for their next edition. That will be harder. As far as I can see, people are not appalled by gutturals or fricatives or spirants, but by meanings; the only word with an ugly meaning that I will agree is beautiful is "diarrhea."

But though I cannot provide you with my favorite word, I can indeed mention the one that is preoccupying me at the moment—one I consider to be worth your prayerful consideration. It is "velleity" (L. *velle,* to wish). Velleity is the lowest

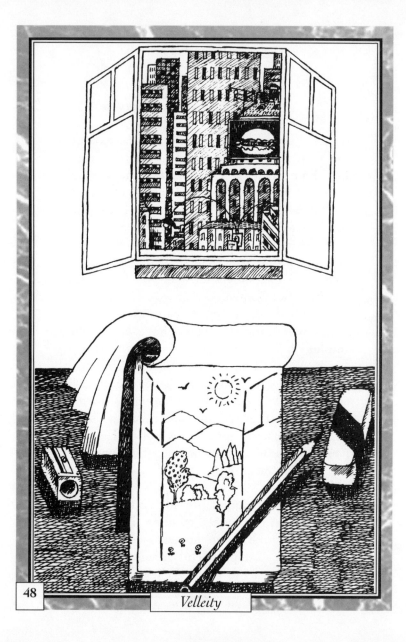

Velleity

degree of desire, the slightest of wishes, the faintest of hopes. It is an inclination so near to none that it will never be acted on; and any disappointment at not acquiring the object so inertly desired will be as faint as the desire was. The lotus eaters had more get up and go to them than velleitists have. At any moment they may not bother to take the next breath, and it will take an autopsist a long time to decide whether they are alive or dead. "Velleity" is one of the saddest words in the world.

Gloria Estefan
(Singer)

My three favorite words are "houndation," "weirdness," and "plethora."

Douglas Fairbanks, Jr.
(Actor)

I have read your request for "my favorite words" and would be delighted to give you a few of mine. I have listed them in no particular order and chosen them because of their meanings, sounds, and uses.

rush	chases	shoulder
ruffle	five	shun
round	gesture	thorn
royal	heaven	thee
shame	languid	thou
sure	lazy	thine
surely	mentor	vine
velvet	money	wine
violin	noun	wisdom
wisteria	owl	yes
Aswan Dam	pheasant	zeal
ashes	query	zealous
sugar	hush	

Barbara Silberdick Feinberg

(Author, Words in the News:
A Student's Dictionary of American
Government and Politics)

"Tachyon."

While I do not usually walk around spouting
Greek words like the Oracle at Delphi, I have
been known on more than one occasion to mention "tachyons," from the Greek for "swift." It is
my favorite word because it is so closely associated with my late husband, Columbia University
physicist Gerald (Gary) Feinberg. He coined the
term to describe hypothetical particles that travel
faster than the speed of light. Gary, a normally
cautious driver on Earth's streets and highways,
refused to slow down when contemplating the
prospect of interplanetary travel beyond the con-
fines of our solar system. In the theory of special
relativity, Einstein had reasoned that nothing in
the universe could exceed the velocity of light,
186,000 miles per second. In order to evade this
universal speed limit, Gary reexamined Einstein's
equations and decided that they did not preclude
the existence of faster-than-light particles. As a
dedicated scientist and a devotee of science fiction, he simply would not allow himself to be
"hemmed in" by the speed of light.

With his usual clarity of thought and precise

phrasing, Gary patiently explained the concept of tachyons to this nonscientist over dinner one night in 1967. Unlike Lois Lane, I quickly realized that the gentle professor in tweed jacket, bow tie, and glasses I was dating was actually Superphysicist in disguise. I marveled at his breadth of knowledge and knew almost at once that I wanted to share his vision of the future. Who could resist a man who used his immense intellectual gifts to anticipate hyperspeed space travel and communication with other life-forms. Gary made many important contributions to theoretical physics before and after his yet undiscovered fast-moving particles, but of all his work, they linger in the mind, if not on the tongue. Of course, "tachyon" is not a word I can use in daily life. I wouldn't dare apply it to postal deliveries or supermarket checkout counters. Nevertheless, the cast members of *Star Trek: The Next Generation* are doing their best to add it to our vocabulary, and I'm glad.

Bruce Feirstein

(Author, Real Men Don't Eat Quiche)

Writers traffic in words.

Admittedly, there are those who would argue that our real currency is ideas.

But words—and the ability to strike them together into cogent sentences and paragraphs—words are what separate us from the guys who came up with SaladShooters, Keogh plans, bungee jumping, and steel-cage fight-to-the-death tag-team professional wrestling matches.

The words I like best are onomatopes or onomatopoetic: words that sound like what they describe. "Thunder." "Lightning." "Earthquake," "mud slide," "sonic boom." (On the other hand, maybe I'm just a sucker for the Great Creator's special effects.) I like "oleaginous" (as in "another oleaginous investment banker"), because it sounds slick; the word "obligatory" (it rolls off the tongue like a Mosler safe), plus "titanic" and "tectonic plates." (I'm not sure why, but to my ears, they just sound massive.) I also admire "lube job" (possibly because it sounds vaguely obscene) and "flotilla." Especially "flotilla." For me, it evokes tall ships, billowing sails, and an armada cutting through the mist at dawn. (Of all the sentences I've written, I think my favorite is "A flotilla of sleepy-eyed limousines cruised up Madison Avenue.")

Winston Churchill once said that "old words are best, and short words are best of all."

My single favorite word meets both these criteria. I enjoy hearing it most in response to the following questions.

"Will you publish the book?"

"Will it be on the best-seller list?"

"Will it make a million dollars?"

And that word, of course, is:

"Yes."

Gary Fisketjon
(Editor, Alfred A. Knopf, Inc.)

"Arete" (from the Greek).

Milos Forman
(Film director)

When I came to America for the first time, all English words sounded to my ear equally nonsensical, but one sounded more nonsensical than the others and that is probably why I developed a strange fondness for it and started to use it quite often.

This word not only expressed with great accuracy the level of my English, but with the same accuracy also described the expressions on the faces of my listeners: "discombobulated."

Richard Frances
(Director of Psychiatry,
Hackensack Medical Center; general editor,
A Clinical Textbook of Addictive Disorders)

I nostalgically love the words "hermeneutics" and "vicissitudes." Hermeneutics is the science of interpretation, which psychoanalysts and psychiatrists like to take as their special purview. Vicissitudes are the changes that occur in one's narcissism in relation to self and others that keep life interesting. In the heyday of psychoanalysis, there was little question that interpretation was a science and little question about who knew best how to interpret. The vicissitudes of narcissism were on every psychiatrist's lips at meetings, though the word never would be used with patients. In fact, in those days we didn't talk that much with patients; we listened, and when we did speak, we avoided highfalutin jargon. In the era of Jane Brody, the consuming public has grown expert, there is less need for biblical scholars to interpret the Bible, and increasingly patients look askance at our noble search for meaning. As for the vicissitudes of our professional self-regard, these are rough times for psychiatrists, who may not have all the answers but who strive for better tools to help patients. Nowadays, Hermes, the caduceus-carrying god who brought scientific messages in the old days only to those with white hair and advanced training, brings hermeneutics to the mass culture; and alas, it is probably better that way.

Lewis Burke Frumkes
(Author, How to Raise Your I.Q. by Eating Gifted Children; Metapunctuation)

My favorite words have changed over the years. When I was a youngster of ten or twelve, for example, reading a lot of romantic novels about knights in shining armor and princesses and things, I was fascinated by the word "gadzooks," which seemed to be the exclamation of choice to evoke in the presence of a dragon, say, or a hydra-headed monster that was blocking your way. I, however, adapted it to fit just about every situation whether it was appropriate or not, "Gadzooks, if it isn't Peter Green," I would say, or "Gadzooks, it's a peanut butter sandwich again today."

Sensational as "gadzooks" was at the time, people grew tired of hearing it two or three hundred times a day, and begged me to abandon it for more sophisticated locutions. So I moved on to "Barsoom," and "Barsoomian," which were the words John Carter of Mars, my hero, discovered were the correct Martian words to describe that faraway planet and its inhabitants. It is amazing how Barsoomian a grapefruit can look when you really think about it, or an ugly friend, or a dog for that matter. To this day my brother calls me Woola in an affectionate way, the name of a Barsoomian dog. (See Roy Frumkes.)

When I began to write professionally some years later, the words "kumquat" and "eggplant" seemed to surface more often in my writing than other words, which was curious (another favorite word) and may have had more to do with the shape of the objects, ovoid, than with their sounds . . . I'm an egg man.

In any event, I am attracted as well to words such as seductive, cute, beguiling, ineluctable, dark, fabled, littoral, apodictic, *mariposa*, *Schmetterling*, moor, and redolent, for some reason, and to magical words such as djinn, mage, fey, oneiric, and enchantment. I frequently lace my discourse with words such as lace, engaging, alluring, dragoon, eloquent, and droll, but see no apparent reason for this other than euphony and, I suppose, the images these words conjure up. While I do love many words in and of themselves for a host of aesthetic reasons, and wonder about other people's favorite words and why they love them (which is the raison d'être for this book), ultimately it is the way one arranges favorite words, juggles them in sequence and context, that determines the rhetorical direction and effectiveness of one's thought and ideas.

Melvin B. Frumkes
(Matrimonial lawyer)

I am delinquent and dilatory, which obviously leads to dangerous defalcations.

Hopefully, you will still be able to use the following pearls and gems of wisdom notwithstanding that which is pronounced belies its meaning and intent.

Yup! My words are "Do it now."

I have those words emblazoned on my desks both in the office and at home and I try, in most cases (except this), to adhere to it.

"Do it now." My children, now all adults, can hear those words in their sleep.

My clients are warned to adhere.

Opposing counsel quake with the thought of

Motions for Enforcement and/or Contempt if the thundering admonition of "Do it now" is not adhered to.

My junior associates, paralegals, clerks, and secretaries all know the rules and rarely dare to stray from the mandatory fiat.

The words "Do it now" have served me well, enabling me to meet all kinds of deadlines (that is, all those on which I am able to get an extension), which usually accomplishes wonderful results in the acrimonious litigation in which I am involved.

Roy Frumkes

(Filmmaker/screenwriter, teacher, editor,
The Perfect Vision *magazine)*

I asked the book's author if nicknames counted, and he decided they did. Which is good, because although I love sensual, melifluous words like "melifluous," I always feel a little pretentious using them, which skims the cream off them (as in Brown Cow yogurt), and I like cream with my words.

I've had only a few close friends and family members during my life, and their nicknames are precious to me. When I was young, for instance, my father, for some unknown reason called me "Yussel." When I hit my early teens, I started calling *him* "Yussel." I must have done it religiously, or with some extraordinary sense of conviction, because it stuck. Eventually people who scarcely knew my father were calling him Yussel. By the time I reached my twenties, I rarely even associated myself with its inspiration. On the few occasions when his real name — Harry — would be mentioned, it sounded all wrong. He didn't look like a Harry. He looked like a Yussel. Then I learned that Harry had been a nickname given him by his fifth-grade teacher. His real name was William.

My closest friend for twenty-five years was Robert Janes Winston. When I met him in the eighth grade, he had already been dubbed "Winnie" by his playmates. I picked up the gauntlet. Over the years we did some screenwriting together, and one idea — *The Comeback Trail* — ended up being directed by a filmmaker named Harry Hurwitz. One day Harry asked me why I called Winnie by that name. I tried to explain. He came down on me pretty hard about using nicknames, insisting the practice was childish, etc. Later, a friend of his named Martin Smith visited the office, and I heard Harry calling him "Smitty." What's more, he spotted me hearing him calling him Smitty, looked as if he'd been caught doing something wrong and childish, and from then on always addressed his friend—at least in front of me—as Martin. I just went right on calling Winnie "Winnie."

As to my older brother, the renowned humorist who so kindly invited me to contribute to this book, the moniker he's had to live with for many years is "Woola," from *A Princess of Mars* by Edgar Rice Burroughs, Woola being a six-legged Martian dog of great size, ferocious demeanor, and devoted heart. None of these attributes had anything to do with why my brother ended up saddled with the name. Well, maybe the great size . . . (just kidding, Woola!). I think if it evolved from anything, it was a failed anagram. "Woola" rearranged should spell "Lewis." It doesn't, but the good intentions are there.

Actually, there is one attribute of the Martian Woola which does, coincidentally, fit my brother, and that is the good heart. Surely this must be true, considering all the "Woola"'s he's had to endure, many of them even in public.

Cristina Garcia

(Author, Dreaming in Cuban)

"Piglet"—because I love diminutives and English, unlike Spanish, is so lacking in them.

"Hamlet"—ditto and because we Cubans take our roast pork seriously.

Howard Gardner

(Harvard educational psychologist, and author who introduced and popularized the notion of "multiple intelligences")

It turns out that I care the most about little words and, most especially, about that delightful particle "yet." Most of my writing harbors on the academic, and so I am usually arguing in favor of, or against, some point of view. To begin, I like to set up a tenable counterargument or strawperson, one that has at least surface plausibility. At that point, *"yet"* enters the picture, along with its cousins *"however,"* but in contrast, or that lovely sentence opener: "And yet."

In addition to its compact size, its decisive sound (so reminiscent of the Russian *nyet*), and its hint of optimism, "yet" also documents how much work can be accomplished by a simple concatenation of three letters. It is the family of "yet"—but, and, indeed, moreover, therefore, notwithstanding—and their numerous relatives which permit us to continue arguments, to signal readers about where we have been, where we are going, and how one should feel about each point along the voyage. They supply needed lights in a sea of dark prose.

Most of my fights with copy editors occur around these little words. Some copy editors don't like them at all; some do not want to use them to signal a change of direction; some have their favorite conjunctions and interjections, which happen not to coincide with mine. If I ever challenge a copy editor to a duel, it will probably be prompted by a dropped "yet" or a mangled "in the event."

I lay no claim to be the first to signal the power of these little words. After all, Paul Pierre Broca identified an entire variety of aphasia that features the deletion of these words; Shakespeare's most famous soliloquy begins with six little words, five of them consisting of only two letters each; and I understand that an entire doctoral dissertation has been written on the meaning of the formidable German particle *doch*. And yet, if I am not among the first, I hope that I may be counted among the most faithful advocates of "yet."

Murray Gell-Mann

(Nobel Prize in physics, 1969; author,
The Quark and the Jaguar)

"Quark." See *Calvin and Hobbes,* 1993.

Tom Gerety

(President, Amherst College)

Tough question. I love so many words—"profligate" is a tempting candidate. My favorite words have changed from year to year. As a child, I was fascinated by words whose letters impressed me: "exquisite" (why not "ex-quiz-it," as I once spelled it in a bee), "colonel" (whence the "r"), "geography" (which I fretfully and incorrigibly mispronounced gee-O-grafee). Gardening has given me many of my now favored words: "volunteer" for a plant that comes into my ground on its own, "dirt," "fastigiate," "monoecious," and many others. My favorite word, today, is "variegated" or "variegate," for a leaf with a surprising mix of colors other than green—pinks, whites, yellows, reds.

Dick Gilbert

(CEO, Zena Jeans)

My favorite words are any which start with the three letters *m, o,* and *n,* in that order and no other. Words might come to mind: "Mongolia," "mononucleosis," and perhaps even "monogamy." However, in spite of their venerable beginnings, these words somehow miss the spot.

Examples, examples, I hear. Let's try "moneybags" for starters. As it rolls from my mouth, it makes a great sound. And what could be better—"moneymaker," which *ooh,* sends chills up and down my spine. As I am now on a roll, I imagine "moneygrubber," which also rings my bell. But as in all things in life, the simpler the better, ergo "money," "money," m-o-n-e-y. While some might say bucks, dinero, smackers, dough, or moolah, I simply say money. What other word makes the palms of your hands itch when you know you are going to get some. Although it cannot grow on trees, it sure does make the world go smoothly around.

Penn Gillette

(Entertainer, magician, Penn & Teller)

"Ruckus" is my favorite word.

Nikki Giovanni

(Poet, playwright, Cypress, Sassafras & Indigo;
For Colored Girls)

If by "favorite" we mean the word we most use, then mine clearly is "illogical." There is, of course, no reason to think human beings should be logical, but the optimist in me insists, thereby forcing me to conclude: illogical when the unacceptable intrudes. On the other hand, my happiest word is "moile," which is really not a word but a feeling. When I am happy, I feel like a happy moile. A moile looks like a who with a Santa Claus laugh. Good things come from moiles. I wrote a poem about it.

Sheldon Glashow

*(Mellon Professor of the Sciences, Harvard
University, Nobel Prize winner, physics)*

Professionally, "charm" is my beloved because I used it to characterize the fourth quark flavor long before it was found. It is indeed a device to ward off evil, if by "evil" is meant a conflict between experiment and theory.

"Radii" and "skiing" both have double *i*'s, but only "hajji" does it for *j*. No English word competes with German *Schneeeule*, since "head-mistress-ship" is hyphenated. "Indivisibility" has more *i*'s than any other word I know except its plural, which has seven. Finally, can you find a word longer than "assesses" containing no string of three different letters?

Harrison J. Goldin

(Former comptroller, City of New York)

I love words, all words, the very idea of words — their precision, their color, their subtlety, their sound. But I have special associations with some that distinguish them from all the others and evoke a particular thought or recollection.

Most of all there is "hereon," not for its euphony or clarity or romance, but because it reminds me of an occasion. Years ago, when I was much younger and before our children were born, on a beautiful summer Sunday afternoon, my wife, Diana, and I would sometimes take a leisurely spin on our motorcycle along country roads near our home in Dutchess County. The rides were exhilarating—the warm breeze at our faces, she holding on to me tight, the beautiful scenery, the joy of intimacy between us and nature. One such day, as the miles sped by, I turned my head to her slightly and, as she leaned in to listen, said, "Have you ever heard of this guy Here-e-on? He must be the biggest landowner in the Hudson Valley!" Sure enough, on every "posted" sign we passed (the ones that warn trespassers to keep off private property) was prominently displayed (on nearly every other tree) the name of the apparent proprietor, always in big black letters, "Hereon." I racked my brain; we conferred. We knew that Roosevelts, Vanderbilts, Morganthaus, even lesser lights of our acquaintance were large landowners in the area. But a Mr. "Hereon"? Perhaps a mysterious Wall Street tycoon, or a South American. Pronouncing it "Here-e-on," as we did, made it seem vaguely Scottish or even Celtish. Suddenly, we both slapped our foreheads at the same time, feeling simultaneously foolish. I stopped the motorcycle and read aloud. "No trespassing," the sign said in small letters, "HEREON," in thick, black bold ones. The secret tycoon was unmasked, the mystery solved.

From that day to this, whenever I meander on country lanes and see posted land, I remember that lovely day, how perplexed I had been and how silly I felt. Mr. Here-e-on indeed!

Al Goldstein
(Founder/publisher, Screw *magazine)*

"Chocolate" and/or "Bangkok."

Edward Gorey
(Cartoonist, creator/illustrator of the opening credits for Mystery *on PBS; author,* Amphigorey; The Curious Sofa)

My favorite word is "silence"; it would be perverse to go on.

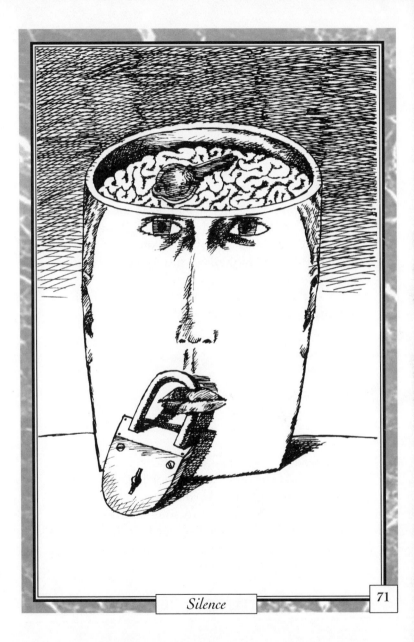

Silence

Virginia Graham

(Actress, television personality)

I have always been a devotee of outrageous and explicit hyperbole, and an adjective has a release from too many social restraints.

So, as we get more mature (I hate the word "older"), I have substituted such words as:

"I find this 'exceedingly inappropriate'"; "inappropriate" might be used instead of "How could you invite three former wives to your party?"

"I think you looked so much better before your face adjustment."

"Some people lose all their looks when they get fat."

All may be true, but inappropriate.

Roger Granet

(Poet/psychiatrist)

The music of words makes my heart sing. In particular, when the melody of a word expresses the lyric, it achieves lexical harmony.

I guess, I'm just a fool for onomatopoeia. Being asked to choose favorite words is like asking a parent to choose special children among many—instant ambivalence is precipitated.

However, for the sake of brevity, I'll try to select a few whose noise captures their meaning:

"Ebullient," "effervescent," and "effusive"— those SAT standards, communicate hopeful energy.

"Cacophony" shouts, while "gossamer" whispers. "Sonorous" sounds rich and deep, as "tenacious" has the resonance of gritty determination.

"Nidus" has the ring of a new start, "hubris" an auditory swagger.

And it seems to me that the German language has a unique capacity to capture dysphoria— *Angst* (anxiety) and *Weltschmertz* (world disgust or melancholia) are serious sounds of psychic discomfort.

And of all the words I studied in medical school, none have greater poetic pitch than the triplet "ontogeny recapitulates phylogeny." As best I can recall, the phrase means that the development of an embryo parallels Darwinian evolution—but that's irrelevant. Just say it out loud a few times and tell me it doesn't suggest a pleasant nursery school rhyme.

I would be remiss in my list if I didn't add my least favorite word: "love." How could such a mundane monosyllabic collection of consonants and banal vowels attempt to symbolize the most spectacular amalgam of emotions? The future awaits a creative reorchestration of the alphabet, to provide a neologism for "love." Now, that would be a symphony, even to the ears of the most "unctuous misanthrope"!

Alan "Ace" Greenberg
(CEO, Bear Stearns & Co.)

"Omphaloskepsis."

Dan Greenburg
(Author, How to Be a Jewish Mother; Exes)

"Basically": Since I was a senior in college, whenever I've wished to parody the fatuous, the pretentious, or the pedantic, I have interjected the word "basically" into almost every phrase. Needless to say, I also interject the word "basically" whenever I'm being fatuous, pretentious, or pedantic myself.

"Peppy": When Carl Reiner and Mel Brooks first came out with the "2,000 Year Old Man" record albums, my buddies and I listened to them so often, we soon had the routines committed to memory. Brooks's use of the word "peppy" insinuated itself into my speech and into my writing, where it remained for many years.

"Guy": I have always liked the informality of the word "guy," and tend to use it a bit more than I should.

Basically, I guess I'm just a peppy guy.

A. R. Gurney, Jr.

(Playwright, Love Letters, A Cheever Evening*)*

"Avuncular"—because it seems to describe my behavior these days.

Mark Hamill

(Actor, Luke Skywalker in Star Wars*)*

One word that made a lasting impression on me is one I've never heard in everyday conversation. It was in a wonderful movie I saw with my family when I was perhaps eight or nine years old and seemed to contain a sense of magic and wonder that makes me smile to this very day.

The word? "Pixilated."

I have been dividing people into and out of this specific category ever since.

And yes—I am. Are you?

Helen Handley
(Poet, anthologist)

Words combined—phrases, sentences, paragraphs, and pages—give me such a boost! But there's the isolated word, also, which, like unaccompanied music, has its own surprises of tone and resonance. My favorite word is "serendipity"; it sounds springy, full of good luck, whooptee! Thanks to Horace Walpole, who gave us serendipity: happy accidents and unexpected discoveries; looking for one thing, we find another, which is what we really wanted all along. I also like "smooth," "enshrine," "bouquet." "Words exhale temperament," said the late Howard Moss. So there's something of mine.

Don Hauptman
(Author, Cruel and Unusual Puns;
Acronymania)

One of my favorite words is "festoon."
The proposal for my first book, *Cruel and Unusual Puns*, contained this sentence: "As a wicked parody of the excesses of academic journalese, I

intend to festoon the Introduction with pseudo-scholarly footnotes and deconstructionist analysis."

Every time the word came up in discussions with my agent, we broke into laughter, chuckles, and guffaws. And why not? Certainly, "festoon" has an amusing sound, suggesting "festive" (to which it is related) and such "fun" words as "balloon," "bassoon," "buffoon," and "cartoon."

As things turned out, the particular festooning I had envisioned did not occur. But *Cruel* was a success, launching my second writing career, as an author of books on language and wordplay. Were I superstitious, I might have convinced myself that the word served as a good-luck charm.

"Festoon" derives, via French, from the Italian *festone*, literally a decoration for a feast *(festa)*. Its original meaning (a noun) is "a string or garland, as of leaves or flowers, suspended in a loop or curve between two points" *(American Heritage Dictionary*, third edition). "Festoon" subsequently came to mean a decorative reproduction of such a device, as, for example, an ornament in painting, sculpture, or architecture. The sense was then extended to other curved or scalloped shapes, such as an arrangement of fabric.

After checking a few dictionaries for this assignment, I concluded that my use of the word in the book proposal was more liberal than literal. But as a verb, in current parlance, I suspect that one can metaphorically festoon just about anything, simply by placing generous quantities of an item on or in it.

So don't just sit there. Go out and festoon something today!

Jack Hausman

(Cofounder, United Cerebral Palsy; past chairman, Belding-Heminway Corporation)

"Fabulous." How I feel when I'm with good *friends.* When asked about my golf *game.*

Naura Hayden

(Author, How to Satisfy a Woman Every Single Time; Astrological Love)

I love funny words. "Tumleys" is possibly my favorite word, or maybe "duckum" or "derangel." These are my made-up words for the love of my life. Because he has a *great* sense of humor and we laugh a *lot,* particularly at silly things, I sometimes say "Tumleys is my derangel (and you *are* deranged!)", and that leads to some *really* silly stuff from him (he's much funnier than I, and you now may be thinking, well, *that* wouldn't be too difficult), but after rereading this, I think my *all-time* favorite word would be "goodness."

Maida Heatter
(Cookbook writer)

My favorite word is "chocolate." It's the most delicious word I know. Some scientists may question this, but there are millions of chocolate lovers who will vouch for the fact that eating chocolate makes them feel sixteen years old and madly, head-over-heels in love. And there are those who claim that it will cure whatever ails you. The word—if I read it or write it or say it—tastes just great to me.

Florence Henderson
(Actress, The Brady Bunch; *host, United Cerebral Palsy Telethon)*

What a great idea! I have now become totally obsessed with words. Following are a few of my favorites:

"Misnomer" "misconception"—because people always get them confused.

"Humanity"—because I worry there isn't enough in the world right now.

"Energy"—because it represents a joy in living—a life force.

"Spirit"—it makes me think of grace and compassion and it gives one the faith that they cannot be defeated in life!

"Exacerbate"—it sounds like something you do alone in the bathroom!

I also like "communication," "dedication," and "consecration." By this time I think you know why.*

*Editor's note: Florence is referring to the United Cerebral Palsy Telethon, for which she and Dennis James have worked tirelessly and unselfishly for many years as performers and hosts.

Tony Hendra

(Humorist, author, Going Too Far;
editor, Spy Magazine)

My favorite word is *schmuck.*

When I came to New York in 1964, *schmuck* was the first American word I heard that made me laugh out loud. Even before I knew its literal meaning, I loved this word. And since the only people I knew back then were Jewish, I heard it a lot.

It's not just as a put-down. It evokes the warmth and friendliness of those who helped me come to America, who fed me, set me up and showered me with presents, who bounced me around from one noisy, funny family to another, showed me the ropes in the city of my dreams, taught me to be a New Yorker, like them an easy touch under a hard-boiled exterior, and most important when to yell, drawl, snap, mutter, or simply sigh, "You *schmuck*!"

As a put-down, though, it's perfection. Unlike its hard-edged fricative and plosive Anglo-Saxon cousins, "schmuck" has a gentler, resigned quality to it. "Sure," it seems to be saying, "you exhibit a massive resemblance to the male sexual organ, but at least you're not a *putz.*"

❖ ❖ ❖

Bob Hope

(Comic, actor, national treasure)

My favorite word of all time is "laughter," and when I am asked why . . . I reply, why not?

A. E. Hotchner

(Author, Hemingway and His World;
King of the Hill: A Memoir)

I am increasingly partial to the word "philanthropy." By Webster's definition: "A desire to help mankind as indicated by acts of charity, service, gifts, etc.; love of mankind." It is a word that encompasses an act as simple as taking a bundle of clothes to the Goodwill or as complex as donating ten million to a university. Hemingway once said, speaking of his own philosophy, that "You don't own anything until you give it away." "Philanthropy" is a word that defines that act: reading for the blind; devoting hours to Literacy Volunteers; giving blood; donating a sum to the local hospital, your alma mater, AIDS research, whatever cause concerns you. For the past twelve years, Paul Newman and I have had the good fortune of running a prospering good company that generates millions of dollars of profit every year, every penny of which we give away at year's end to a wide variety of needy causes, ranging from cancer research to field schools for the children of migrant workers. We are blessed with this largesse of philanthropy and I never tire of hearing the word or seeing it on the printed page.

Arianna Huffington

(Author, The Female Woman; The Fourth Instinct; *host, television show,* Critical Mass)

"Trust"; trust in life; trust in God; trust that the Universe is a friendly place; trust that, incredible though it may sound, "not a sparrow falls without His knowing"; trust that there is meaning in our pain and purpose to our lives; trust that we shall meet again; trust that life is a mystery to be lived, not a riddle to be solved—both unutterably sacred *and* the old banana-skin joke on a cosmic scale.

Derek Humphry

(Founder, the Hemlock Society;
author, Jean's Way; Final Exit)

Because most of my life has been devoted to writing and campaigning about civil liberties, my two favorite words are "choice" and "option." Nothing is dearer to me than the right to choose—freedom to read and write, freedom of thought, freedom of religion and from other people's religions, abortion or adoption, life or death (although we don't have any choice about the finality of death, we can sometimes speed it or slow it). If one takes the long view of how Western society is developing, as the traditional shackles on individual behavior evaporate, obviously words like "choice" and "option" will achieve greater usage and significance.

Choice

Evan Hunter

(Author, The Blackboard Jungle; aka Ed McBain, author of more than eighty crime novels, including Mary, Mary)

I've pondered and repondered your question, and for the life of me I cannot think of a favorite word. My favorite color is blue. Does that help?

Susan Isaacs

(Author, Compromising Positions; After All These Years)

I'm fickle. There is no one word to which I've remained faithful. Instead I have relationships that last from a few weeks to a year or two, until I get bored and move on. I've gone from "terrific" to "dandy" and am currently flirting with "swell." I've forsaken "fungible" and "quasi-" and dropped "subanthropoidal" like a hot potato.

Pico Iyer

(Essayist, Time *magazine; author,*
Falling off the Map)

"Languorous." I like the ease, the recline, the slowness that amounts to sensuousness in this word; I like its sense of recumbency, the way it sprawls out like a hammock between the trees, and confounds somehow the casual speller (with its odd—almost unique—conjunction of *uo* and *ou*). I like its liquidity, its looseness, its closeness to all the other lovely *l* words that roll sleepily off the tongue—such as "leisure" and "lulling" and "lithe."

"Languorous" is very much a romance word, a romantic word, a word that belongs in the sun. It has an ugly brother, of course, but "languid" has something clipped about it, sullen and even pouting; "languorous," by contrast, is outstretched and open-hearted. Its Latin cousins, born of the same roots, are "relax" and "release" and "relish," and its very heart—that uncanny "uorou"— sounds like a South Sea love song.

Nothing shocking, you notice, ever happens languorously; nobody ever shouts or agitates languorously. "Languorous" describes the purl of the sea, or the breeze between the palms; it belongs to those enchanted souls who live beyond care or inhibition. Life's pleasures are almost always "languorous," its nightmares almost never.

So it is that the places we dream of are "languorous places," and they call to us like trade winds. "Languorous" involves a sloughing off of time and space, a slipping off of rules, a shedding of hard edges. "Languorous" ushers us, in fact, into a world of sighs.

Rona Jaffe

(Author, The Best of Everything;
Class Reunion)

In my first novel I was partial to the word "whispered," as used in dialogue when one of my girls was asking a question the answer to which she dreaded, such as: "Do you mean you don't love me anymore?" "Whispered" was a humble and frightened word. As I grew older and stronger and my "girls" became women, they began to "say" and "ask." Not that they don't sometimes still dread the answer! I save whispering for a more cheerful context, but use it rarely because it's quite strong. I still think it's a nice word, though, because it sounds like what it does.

Whisper

Dennis James

*(Television personality; host,
United Cerebral Palsy Telethon)*

My life has been full of "skidsomycetees" (little
things with no payoff). I am always pressured by
my wife with "forcenahobbs" (Do this . . . Do
that). It's a "framus" (pain).

Those are three of my words:

"skidsomycetees," "forcenahobbs," and "framus."

Morton Janklow

(Literary agent)

My two favorite words are "windowsill" and
"turquoise." I have no particular psychological
association with these words—I just love the
sound of them.

Tama Janowitz

(Author, Slaves of New York)

I have always liked the words "oolitic limestone."
Dry, friable, slightly sour, and crumbly on the
tongue—something about the name of this rock
reflects what it is exactly. There are also many
other kinds of igneous, metamorphic, and sedi-
mentary rock that I have always thought had appealing names: gypsum, feldspar, slate, schist,
mica, jaspar, and agate are just a few.

Franklyn G. Jenifer

(President, The University of Texas)

One word that I tend to use frequently in both
speaking and writing is "bold." There is something about the very boldness of the word that
appeals to me, i.e., it sounds so much like what it
means. It also has a nice sound to it, with that
full, round *o*.

Often I use the word in the context of what
higher education and other leaders must do to
address the problems that confront them, i.e.,
they must be bold. In a recent speech I gave at a
meeting of the Middle States Association of Colleges and Schools, for instance, I used the word

on several occasions ("higher educational leaders who dare to be bold"; "bold research"; "bold initiatives of productivity"; "we must be bold enough to say to the old guard . . .").

To give another example: Near the end of my opinion piece about the value and validity of predominantly black colleges, published in the October 16, 1991, issue of *The Chronicle of Higher Education,* I wrote:

> Moreover, we must be bold enough to assert—proudly and loudly—that some higher education institutions are predominantly black for compelling historical and sociological reasons, and that, because of those compelling reasons, they should stay that way now and for some time to come.

Somehow I don't think any other word would have done justice to such a bold statement as, yes, "bold."

Richard Johnson

(Columnist, New York Post)

My favorite word, and it's a very useful word, is "merkin."

This word is useful to see if you have a really comprehensive dictionary. A lot of dictionaries just don't have it. The better ones do. The big dictionary in the *Daily News* library has it, and defines it, as "false hair for the pudenda." The word originated in Elizabethan times, and I am informed that it was still in use during the heyday of burlesque when strippers bought merkins from the same salesmen who were peddling G-strings and pasties.

P.S. There was a character in a movie from the late sixties, I believe, named Hieronymous Merkin.

Erica Jong

(Poet, author, Fear of Flying;
The Devil at Large; Fear of Fifty)
Breath, Death, Pillicocks, and Picklocks

In my teens and twenties, in love with language,
I pored over dictionaries and thesauri and made
lists of words like: maenad, mead, pelisse, par-
quetry, viridian, verdancy, rubescence . . . Then I
devised poems in which I could use them. "The
rubescence of the Rubens nudes," I said ruddily
in one line. "Green virility" shimmered elsewhere
on the page. "Parquetries of mellow wood" glow-
ingly seduced the reader's ear and eye. In other
poems maenads went mad in meadows, no doubt
from drinking too much mead, and sprites wore
pink pelisses (perhaps made of flamingo feath-
ers). How reassured I was to find my practice
validated by W. H. Auden in *The Dyer's Hand:* "A
poet has to woo, not only his own Muse, but also
Dame Philology and, for the beginner, the latter
is more important." Aha—when a young poet
loves words above content—it's a good sign.

Words meant so much to me for so long that I
was even moved to write a whole novel in eighteenth-century English, *Fanny Hackabout Jones.*
There I could indulge my word-listings to my
heart's content and still keep the plot moving.
"Pillicock," "picklock," "love-dart" were some of
the terms my heroine used for the masculine

member when she was reduced to whoring in a London brothel circa 1728. Surely some of my delight in writing this novel came from the eighteenth-century language of love itself, which was at once more poetic and blunter than our debased cant for the art of love.

But now, in the middle of my life, I am no longer in love with fancy words. As I feel time's wings beating at my back, I write headlong, trying to use words to get *beyond* words. Perhaps flesh cannot stay, but surely, breath can.

"Breath" is my favorite word today. It is like "flesh," but more ethereal. Like "breast," but even warmer and moister. Like love, it makes us rise. It begins with lips together, but it ends with lips open and the tongue touching the palate's arch. All of life is in this word. And it rhymes with nothing but "death." That should tell us something.

Jenny Joseph

(Poet, The Unlooked-for Season;
Rose in the Afternoon; Persephone)

There are some words that other people have noticed occur quite frequently in my work. "Lure" (the verb) is one; "the sun," "light," and "dark" are others. I am not sure these are my favorite words in the way I would say creme caramel is a favorite dessert. "Air" and "water" are even more essential to life.

"Trombone" and "trumpeter" I like for their sounds, for I love brass bands that used to play on damp late-afternoon autumn Sundays in neglected English towns, and the word "glory" seems somehow to go with them.

Two words for which I find no substitute so they are like prime numbers, irreducible, are "kindness" and "green." An "irreducible" line of John Donne's lingers in my mind: "good is as visible as green."

If my answer to "What is your favorite word?" were honest, I would have to send you my two-volume Funk & Wagnall 1889 dictionary—too precious to part with.

If you must have only one word, it had better be "air."

⊷ ⊷ ⊷

Lure

Bel Kaufman

(Author, Up the Down Staircase)

I offer you four:

The first that comes to mind is "no!" It's a powerful word, which I have begun to use only in my late years, when I realized that I was entitled to speak my mind, that I did not need to be loved or accepted by everyone, and that I had the wisdom to know what I wanted and what I did not want.

By contrast, the word "yes" was one I used when I was young, buying love and acceptance with my compliance. Of course, "no" may have deprived me of some positive offers in my life, and "yes" condemned me to acquiesce to the second-best, but on the whole, I am pleased at my present ability to make a choice.

A word that has always given me great pleasure both for its sound and its evocative quality is "onomatopoeia," and its adjective, "onomatopoetic." It makes me think of *buzzing* bees and *beeping* beeps, and it has a kind of elegance I like.

A fourth word is "cozy." It never fails to make me think of fireplaces and warm blankets and nestling someplace, curled up, snug and warm, with a book or an apple or both. The sound itself is a cozy one: the *o* round and friendly, the *z* easy on the tongue. It almost sings.

Mimi Kazon

(Gossip columnist/writer)

"Effrontery."

The love of my life once said to me, "I find your effrontery charming." I was utterly charmed by him and the word "effrontery."

Every time I hear it, it evokes memories of sex, lies, and the seven hours of his performances I have on videotape.

Edmund Keeley

(Author; director of the Creative Writing Program, Princeton University, ex-President of PEN)

"Licorice" is my word. I like the beginning, middle, and end of it. The beginning is its origin in Greek — my favorite foreign language — where sounds meaning "sweet root" were engendered, suggesting the first of pleasures. Its middle origin is the Latin for "liquor," my favorite hobby after adolescence. Its end is its abiding taste, whether in its pure form, bringing back early memories of molasses and later memories of the sweet tar in cigarettes that one had to give up in middle age, or in its adulterated form as pernot or ouzo, tastes that may linger until the sweet root of it carries the mind beyond sex and indulgence and even memory into that realm where the sound of the word alone will do for a final pleasure.

Gene Kelly
(Actor/dancer, Singing in the Rain)

Herewith are a few of my favorite words.

Like most words, I like to hear them said out loud. I like the sound of them better than seeing them in print.

My favorite: "plethora."
Some others: "blending"
　　　　　　　"siesta"
　　　　　　　"succubus."

Say them out loud . . . they really sing!

Judith Kelman

(Author, The House on the Hill; Someone's
Watching)

My favorite word, no contest, is "serendipity." I
like the feel and sound of it. I enjoy the lingual
challenge, sort of an advanced Step Reebok
workout for the tongue. Above all, I appreciate
the value of serendipity: mining for unexpected
positives in the cosmic pie throw that is life. As
my mother often says, "Rich or poor, it's nice to
have money," but that's for another book.

Serendipitously, when you remove the dip,
you wind up with "serenity." I'll nominate that as
my first runner-up. If, at any time during its
reign, "serendipity" should prove unable to fulfill
its duties, "serenity" will suit me fine.

Rose Kennedy

*(Mother of President John F. Kennedy and Senator
Edward M. Kennedy)*

At 102 years old and very frail, Mrs. Kennedy
responded to my query through her deputy press
secretary, Melody Miller, who said:

"Her favorite word is 'faith.' Considering all
she has been through in her lifetime, I believe

that this word is an understandable choice. Her faith has been the sustaining force in her life."

Victor Kiam

(CEO, Remington Products Company)

"You don't have to teach eagles how to fly."

"Business is where you are."

"No decision is worse than making the wrong decision."

"I liked it [the shaver] so much, I bought the company."

"If you have a lemon, make lemonade."

"Show me someone who has never failed, and I'll show you someone who never tried."

Florence King

(Author, With Charity Towards None)

I like words calculated to bring a blush to a feminist's cheek. I am a "spinster" because I have never married. I am "barren" because I have had the menopause, which is also why I no longer have "affairs": my "desire" is gone. I am not "single" because that can mean anything and usually does; I am not "sterile" because that describes males and I am female; I have never had "relationships" because they sound intolerably earnest, and I have never had a "sex drive" because it sounds as if it belongs in a graph instead of a bed. I believe in using one time-honored word, not two or three faddish buzzwords, that says exactly what I mean and that cannot possibly mean anything else. That way lies "precision"—perhaps my favorite word of all because I can hear the ball bearing rolling through it.

I also love "profanity." My mother was a mule-skinner cusser in the great tradition of the U.S. Cavalry, capable of dazzling cascades and ingenious combinations that put today's unimaginative "obscenity" to shame. Her favorite epithet—"double asshole, shit sandwich, five-alarm turd sonofabitch"—sounds like a 100 mph fastball whizzing down the middle and thudding into the catcher's mitt. Abe Lincoln was right: All that I am or hope to be I owe to my angel mother.

Larry King
(Host, Larry King Live)

My favorite word is "why." I use it more than any other—professionally and otherwise. It begins a lot of my questions and it can't be answered with one word. It's probably the best word in the universe. Think about it.

John Kluge
(Chairman and president, Metromedia Company)

My favorite word is "yes."

Joan Konner
(Dean, Graduate School of Journalism, Columbia University)

My favorite word, this week, is "egg." It's plain. It's simple. It's minimalist. It doesn't waste syllables. It has a beginning and an end and no middle. Nevertheless, it's potentially pregnant. It mates well with other words. Like "lemon." Lemon and egg.

So far, I have only one other word to rival it at

the moment. The word is "dog," for some of the same reasons, but "dog" scampers off in other directions. I'm drawn to one-syllable words.

The word "egg" in a sentence:

An egg is an egg is a chicken.

I can hear the obvious. That laid an egg.

Paul Krassner

(Editor, The Realist; *author,* Confessions of a Raving, Unconfined Nut)

My favorite word is "change," because it is such a catalyst for subjective interpretation. To a clerk at the supermarket, it means "money." To an infant in a shopping cart, it means "diapers." To a shopper waiting on line, it means a new "self-help" program. And to me, it means the very process of "evolution." Also, that I might change my favorite word at any given moment.

Charles Krauthammer

(Essayist, columnist, Time *magazine)*

It turns out that my favorite word is "preposterous." I wasn't aware of this until my wife pointed out the alarming regularity with which I use the word. It seems that I use it to describe most any opinion with which I disagree.

The word has two endearing qualities. First, it is rather gentle, in contrast to, say, "idiotic." Second, it expresses itself without need of translation. It is onomatopoeic. Pre-post-er-ous: Once all the syllables have rolled off the tongue, the word has done its work. What is an opinion thus calumnied to do but slink away in shame?

Bernard Kripke

(Computer scientist)

My favorite words have been stories, such as "bunkum," after the congressional representative who had been blathering on the floor of the House for the benefit of his constituents in Buncombe County, North Carolina. I once lived next door to a descendant of the Pennsylvania farmer who gave his name, "Haymaker," when he struck his neighbor dead with one punch. Another favorite is "hoist with one's own petard"—blown up by one's own explosive device (in French, a fart).

Hedy Lamarr
(Actress, Samson and Delilah; Ecstasy)

"Empathy."

Felicia Lamport
(Poet)

For years I've cherished the word "jejune" because it creates a visual pun that trips up the literati, those who are the most likely to use the word at all. "Jejune" is a simple little word, pronounced as spelled, with a rare two-*j* construction that catches the eye, a gentle little stutter that beguiles the ear, and a meaning of "barren, arid, unsatisfying" that springs etymologically from "jejunum," the small intestine that, when empty, produces precisely that feeling. The image is so vivid that it tempts one to sing, "It's Jejune in JeJanuary."

But the Francophilic literati compulsively see

"jejune" as "jejeune," which naturally induces them to pronounce it "zhezhoon" and define it as "puerile, childish." And they career into this error in such numbers that many modern lexicographers, who take pride in following in the footsteps of the illuminati, sanction this misdefinition, although they illogically retain the correct pronunciation and spelling of the word.

My choice of "jejune," though apparently persnickety, is really an attempt to rescue a fine word from the mire of misuse into which it has fallen.

P.S. "Persnickety" is a subfavorite because it evokes the sound of two ants crossing a marble floor wearing twelve tiny stiletto-heeled shoes.

Ann Landers

(Syndicated columnist)

My favorite word is "chocolate." No question about it, I am addicted.

It would be impossible for me to conquer this addiction because all my friends (and even some strangers) know that I am hooked. Barely a week goes by that I don't receive at least two boxes.

The word "chocolate" has a beautiful sound, and when I hear it, the juices start to flow and I simply must find a piece of Fanny Farmer, Godiva, or Nestlé. If none of these is available, I will settle for those rather ordinary Hershey Kisses.

I suspect that this addiction may be genetic because I have a twin sister on the West Coast who is in the same fix. Neither of us, however, wants to do anything about it because eating chocolate is such fun.

Lewis Lapham

(Essayist, author, editor of Harper's *magazine)*

When I was younger, I wrote a good deal of poetry, most of it in poor imitation of W. H. Auden or Ezra Pound, and I still delight in words for no reason other than their sound. Again for no reason that I can explain, it is the shorter and simpler words that seem to me to hold their place in the dance to the music of time. As follows:

rain
summer
mirth
pear
ruffian
sea
blush
spaniel

rose
Avalon
bawd
crown
dust

Ring Lardner, Jr.
(Novelist; screenwriter, M*A*S*H;
The Cincinnati Kid)

I have always been intrigued by the vast store of obscure words and redundant synonyms in our language, and even in my present state of "caducity" (frailty of old age), I relish some of them for their sound: "glabrous" (smooth, devoid of hair); "susurrus" (gentle murmur, whispering, rustling); "gallimaufry" (jumble, hodgepodge). Others I value because, while not in common use, they have meanings that are relevant and applicable to the world we know: "ergophobia" (fear or hatred of work); "iatrogenic" (caused by a physician, as of a medical disorder); "misology" (hatred or distrust of reason, reasoning, or discussion). I believe much of American public opinion is the result of misology.

Eric Larsen

(Author, Zoe Hanke; An American Dream)

For me, one of the things about words is that there just aren't enough of them. When I was a student at Iowa City—this was back in 1963 or 1964—I heard the Irish story writer Bryan MacMahon say that he hated to let a day go by without learning a new word: anytime he went into a tradesman's shop, or into a store, or saw someone working with anything from machinery to food to animals, he'd stop, get into a conversation, and ask questions until a new word came up that he could carry away with him. Even then, with all his collected words, he constantly had to resist relying too heavily on a few recurring favorites—he mentioned "paten," I remember, as a word he especially loved and had to guard against. Not "paten," but the general problem is the same with me, or sort of: no matter how many words I try to collect, or gather, or hoard, there are never enough to displace the few old needed favorites that come back to beg or sneak their way onto the page. For three decades I've been writing fiction that's got—I think I'm finally beginning to see this—*time* as its driving theme. Time is life, after all, and when time runs out, life is gone, so I think that writing—art—is a compulsive holding action, an attempt at almost any cost to hang on to life by bringing time to a stop.

Take a close look at Hemingway, Faulkner, Virginia Woolf, and that's a big part of what you'll find. But it's a dangerous business, as I know only too well. What are my own words? I don't even have to look back over the pages of my books, because I know perfectly well the familiar words I'll find whispering there as they persist hopelessly in trying to make their escape from time: "poised," "motionless," "quiet," "still," "calm," "hushed," "unmoving," "silent." Maybe one or two others as well, but you can already see the difficulty: my most favored words beckon me toward one logical end—not moving, being silent, saying nothing.

Robin Leach
(Host, Lifestyles of the Rich and Famous)

Alliterations such as "extraordinary excitement," "majestic monied moguls," "born beautiful," etc., etc. I use alliterations both on television and in ordinary conversations because I appreciate words and the way they can dazzle and delight!

David Leavitt
(Author, Legend of the Lost Cranes)

My own favorite word is *madrugar*, a Spanish verb which has no equivalent in English. It derives from *la madrugada*, in Spanish the period between late evening and early morning — roughly, 2 to 6 A.M. To *madrugar* is to go out and behave wildly during the *madrugada*.

Guy Lebow
(Radio broadcaster)

Here, two of my favorite words:

"Notoriety": I've adopted this word. I've learned to protect it because it's used erroneously so often. I hear broadcasters say, "He earned his tremendous notoriety for his incredibly expressive singing voice." Or I read in the paper that so-and-so is "notorious" in his neighborhood for his kind and generous acts. Considering the celebrated persons who were "properly" notorious — like Dillinger, Capone, Genghis Khan, and Lizzie Borden — the word "notorious" (from the noun "notoriety," meaning dirty-rotten-SOB) should be used with more respect.

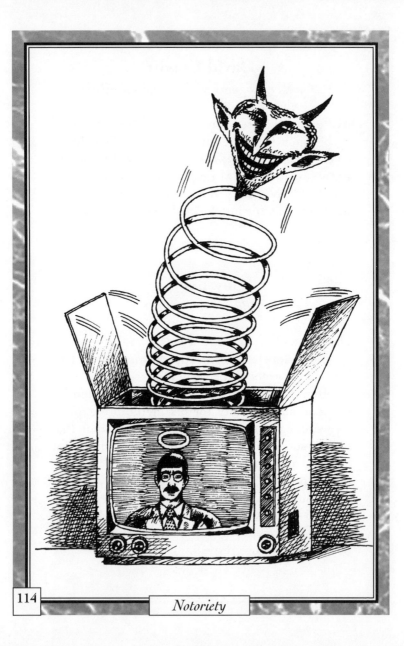

Notoriety

"Tissue" (as in, "Your testimony, sir, is a tissue of lies"): I love this term because it's a grandiloquent way of saying, "Sir (or Madam), you are a liar." The other reason is very personal. When you do the proper English courtroom version, the word "tissue" is pronounced with soft *s*'s—a hiss . . . *"tiss-syoo,"* and it becomes intimidating to the person who is the target. But if you use the American version, the word becomes *"tishyoo,"* as in toilet.

Richard Lederer

(Author, The Miracle of Language; More Anguished English; *and many other best-selling books about language)*

Has there ever been another word as human as "usher"? In sound and meaning it is not a paragon among words, but it contains the full spectrum of humankind. Words and people have always hung around together, and within the brief compass of the five letters in "usher," we find the four pronouns "us," "she," "he," and "her." Like humanity, "usher" has a long history, going all the way back to the Latin *ostium,* "door," related to *os,* "mouth." So there again is that iron link between things and human beings.

"Usher" winkingly reminds us that all words are created by people and that language inevitably reflects the fearful asymmetry of our kind. Even though writers write, bakers bake, hunters hunt, preachers preach, and teachers teach, grocers don't groce, butchers don't butch, carpenters don't carpent, milliners don't millin, haberdashers don't haberdash—and ushers don't ush.

Richard Lefrak
(Real estate developer)

My favorite words are "No Vacancy"!

Elmore Leonard
(Author, Maximum Bob)

My favorite words: "cellar door."

Charles Lindner

(Humorist, lecturer)

"Obit" is my favorite word. It used to be "obituary." But now that I'm a senior citizen, every fraction of a second counts. Also being a humorist and lecturer, I adhere to the adage that "brevity is the soul of wit." In addition, I've noticed that the word "obit" and my profession of making people laugh are closely related. Many a time I've died on stage, killed the audience; or the audience died laughing.

Also, I love reading the "bios" of the rich and famous. The "obit" page of the daily newspaper succinctly says it all: Saves me money, time, and shelf space buying "bios" at the local bookstore.

Reminds me of the story of the widow who wanted to place a two-word notice in the "obit" column of the local paper: "Goldberg died." She was told there was a five-word minimum. "Okay," she replied. "Put in: 'Goldberg died, Cadillac for sale.'"

As ninety-eight-year-old George Burns would say:

> I wake up each morning and dust off my wits;
> I pick up the paper, and check the OBITS;
> If my name is not in it, I know I'm not dead;
> I eat a good breakfast and go right back to
> bed.

George adds, "Even if my name appears in the OBIT column, I'm still gonna have a good breakfast, 'cause I won't leave on an empty stomach."

Art Linkletter
(Radio/TV host, producer)

Some favorite words:

> murmur
> lullaby
> dawn
> consolation
> butterfly

Gordon Lish
(Editor, teacher, author)

Just between you, me, and the lamppost, I guess I probably could be pretty successfully accused of a certain felonious partiality for "that," for "which," and for "whereas." Not (gee, "not," "not"—hey, isn't that a honey for you right there, not to mention, hard by, the old voluptuary, "a," itself?) that I ever would dare ever to ever confess to such an avidity—ever! ever!—in a place that is this (actually, give me a "this" over a "that" any day of the week, you know?) public. Look, so far as my shooting my mouth off for the record goes, suppose we just say this—that I am willing to be dead-set against any word that looks as if it might want to give even preliminary evidence of its wanting to keep on squatting around making an issue of its sovereignty, all smugly preoccupied out of all proportion with its not ever being susceptible to its ever being genial to the idea of its ever goddamn succumbing to anyone's ever wanting to deform it, which is why, for your information, the more vacant the word—the blanker, the more detachable—the more likely I am likely to be prepared to go ahead and give it a tumble, given that less of anything laden with otherness can maybe keep on getting away with its still being so viciously and so maliciously and so antilishiously stuck to it. Ah, but who's kidding who? Words? Count on it—there is not one blessed one of them that, given half a chance, wouldn't come rushing in and commit homicide—or just as bad, get you killed for it.

Phillip Lopate

(Writer, essayist; author, "Against Jove de Vivre," "The Art of the Personal Essay")

"Austere" has been a favorite word of mine since my movie-mad adolescence, when it rhymed, sort of, with "auteur." It conjures up the cold Danish hush of Carl Dreyer films, Puritan pastors moving through white-walled rooms in black garb; a formalist necessity, inevitability, severity in art that thrilled me when I came to understand it. I doted on the sternness of Piero della Francesca, Dürer, Mondrian, Bach, Bresson, Webern. As it turned out, I did not become a particularly austere writer, but one who treats words as intrinsically impure, multipliable, to be used unceremoniously and not worshiped. But I still shudder a little when I see the onomatopoeic "austere." The first syllable raises its hand like a traffic cop, stops us in awe, freezes us like the glint of gold (au). The second trembles un-Englishly between the sound of "steer" (castration-fear), "stir," and "stare." I like that: awe-stare, stare in awe at this simple, grave construction. A consecrated space. The Rothko Chapel.

Yet "austere" also carries in its wake the shadow of Astaire, that most graceful, seemingly unRothko-ish performer. Still, beyond Fred's technical perfection, is not what we cherish about him his austere devotion? That severe,

120

Austere

121

bony face and thinning hair, so far from the handsome, sulky luxuriance of Gable and other male stars, and when he danced, he wasn't sexy, or even trying to be, like Kelly, but economical, hieratic, addressed to a concentrated mysterious perfection of the line, trimming away all Rubensesque fat or blur.

"Austere" conveys the ascetic pleasures of sublimation and restraint. I have also been partial in my time to "rigorous," "intransigent," and "recalcitrant." All these circle around the concept of Limit. Others chafe at limit; I relax into it. When I do not set limits for myself, I find them all too easily within myself. Part of my love of "austere" and a morality of borders can be explained as a reaction to my chaotic childhood. My operatic mother monopolized emotion, giving it a hysterical cast (but then, "hysteria" and "austere" are not so far apart in sound, suggesting a buried, doppelgänger relationship). My father, on the other hand, was somber, grave, and infuriatingly withdrawn. It has been my yearning to cultivate a third path, a calm interiority and outward gregariousness, in which emotion still burns, albeit with an austere, controlled flame.

"Austere" also brings to mind "wisteria." Such is my limited knowledge of the plant kingdom that I am unable to summon any image of that species, though its name has a plaintively wistful suggestiveness, and one can never have too much wistfulness.

Shirley Lord
(Author, My Sister's Keeper; *beauty director,* Vogue *magazine)*

I know my husband has been far more "punctilious" about responding to your fascinating letter, which is embarrassing as I am very fond of the word and realize in my books that words beginning with the letter *p* appeal to me — "powwow," "pulchritude," and — yes — "punctuate," too. Beats me as to why, but there it is.

Robert Ludlum
(Author, The Icarus Agenda; The Osterman Weekend, The Scorpio Illusion)

"Dissembler" — Such a soft-sounding word that connotes such evil — which, I suspect, was why it was one of Shakespeare's favorites in the area of villainy.

"Savant"—Certainly not in everyday usage, but it conveys a person of overwhelming yet mysterious access to knowledge. Fascinating!

"Resplendent"—Roget's gives it three classifications: "bright," "gorgeous," "illustrious." I think it's all three and then some. For me it also speaks of posture, dignity, even morality in the best sense, if you like.

Roa Lynn
(Author, Learning Disabilities)

I like a word that embodies its meaning within its sound, dances and somersaults within its sound. "Shimmer" is an example. Other wonderful words: cringe, tinkle, grimace, farrago, thump, squirt, mumble, wisp. The sound unlocks an imagined scene, the sound puts me in the action, tells me what to be suspicious of and what to believe in. It's not just onomatopoeia—maybe you need to know English to know what these words mean, but they could all be acted out by amateurs and the speaker of Portugese or Turkish would understand. They are "sound glimpses," perhaps into a room that has no fourth wall.

Yo-Yo Ma
(Cellist)

After much deliberation in my office as to what my favorite words are, I have come to two choices. The first, "genuine"; the second, "incredible."

I use the word "genuine" a lot because it marks a subject or an object of integrity and sincerity, which are qualities I consider to be absolutely necessary in whatever one does.

I find that an unconditional love of life, and a continual quest for knowledge and new ideas, are what keep me motivated. For this reason I often find myself using superlatives. I find that life is "wonderful," "terrific," "unbelievable," and particularly, "incredible."

I genuinely hope that this is what you are looking for, and that your book turns out to be an incredible success.

Sirio Maccioni
(Owner, Le Cirque restaurant, New York)

"LIFE." Sirio Maccioni's favorite word!

Pamela McCorduck

(Author, Machines Who Think;
The Universal Machine)

"Frog." What a friendly, endearing word for a friendly, endearing creature. It's nice in German too: *Frosch.* It appears as a nickname in our household in both languages, though usually with the diminutive: *"Froggie." Fröschlein.* (The cover of the Manhattan Yellow Pages claims "Frog Dealers" as a category of listings, but look inside and you're disappointed: from "Freight Forwarding" to "Frozen Foods" in one hop.) "Fluid" is another word that seeps into my conversation and writing with unusual frequency. "Frugal." *F*-words. They could begin a friendly kiss.

I'm drawn to other words too: "glamour," for instance. That seems a very 1930s word, evoking platinum blondes and top hats, silver fox furs and Art Deco. The love affair was sealed when I read its etymology, deriving from *gramarye*—enchantment, magic—and brought to modern attention by Bobby Burns: "Ye gipsy gang that deal in glamour/And you deep-read in hell's black grammar/Warlocks and witches . . ."; its roots to be found in the Indo-European *gerbh*—scratch or carve—and so related to a host of writing words: "epigraph," "autograph," "graffiti," and "grammar."

I'm partial to "snuggle." To "architectonic." To "celestial." To "mantissa," a mathematical term I don't quite understand, so can't drop it casually in conversation. Still, if I were an aristocrat, I'd like to be the Countess of Mantissa.

Patrick McGrath
(Author, Spider; Dr. Haggard's Disease)

As an inky-fingered English schoolboy with a great deal more interest in the frog in my pocket than the contents of a Hillard and Botting grammar, Latin *or* Greek, I was skeptical about the benefits of a classical education. What on earth (I muttered) could be the point of studying *dead languages?* Conjugations and declensions, pluperfect tenses, subjunctives, gerundives, and infinitives—I'd have dumped the lot in a minute.

Wiser counsels prevailed. When I closed a Hillard and Botting for the last time, huge, stodgy lumps of those despised dead languages had been thoroughly stuffed into my head, never to be forgotten or dislodged. There they lay, festering in some neglected mental cellar, until, at an advanced age, and in a state of near-desperation, I turned to fiction as my last best hope of earning a living.

Then at last I got it. Words, beautiful words—

the more classical in origin, the better I liked them. "Omnivorous." "Magnanimous." "Concupiscent." "Pantechnion." Large words that broke down into smaller words, yielding their meaning in the process. "Callipygian"—having beautiful buttocks! "Microcephalic"—having an abnormally small head! "Hydrostatics"—the science of fluids at rest! What joy, to bring forth these glorious mouthfuls, though what, for me, was truly exciting was the slowly dawning realization that one could *make them up oneself.*

"Umbrelliferous"—holding an umbrella, as in "She experienced considerable stiffness in her umbrelliferous arm."

"Phlegmosaurian"—concerning a dinosaur whose bones were dug up slightly charred, as in "A passionate argument erupted over the Phlegmosaurian thighbone."

"Bibulophiliac"—one who likes a drink, as in "No Bibulophiliacs."

We owe it to the English language to give it a word or two during the few brief, fleeting moments we're privileged to use it. What better resource than the dead languages that are its soil, its compost? And this, finally, I suggest, is the real point of studying the classics. They facilitate "necrolinguistic neologizing."

Ian MacKenzie

(Managing director, Intermarket Corp.)

"Plastics"!

Ed McMahon

(TV personality, The Tonight Show;
Star Search)

I find your project very interesting. For years I have been a big W. C. Fields fan and have done a poor imitation of him. He was fond of words that could be used to exemplify his style of speaking. I have picked that up. For example, Fields would say something like: "How fortuitous"; "The lovely digits of your beautiful hand have captured my heart. Allow me to participate."

He was always using words to propel his comedy. I find I'm using words that have to do with success. Words like: "endeavor," "persevere," and "continuity." Words that have something to do with getting there, striving successfully, reaching your goals. Anything to do with words like that pleases me.

Norman Mailer

(Author, The Armies of the Night;
Harlot's Ghost)

"Resonance," "dread," and "presence" are, I fear, the words I call upon all too often.

Robert Manning

(Author, The Swamp Root Chronicles:
Adventures in the Word Trade;
former editor, The Atlantic)

I often use "beguiling" in its favorable sense, meaning entertaining or charming, because it has a pleasant sound, compliments without gushiness, and reserve stronger words such as "superb" or "marvelous" or "masterly" for circumstances that truly deserve them.

"Flaccid" is not a pleasant word, either in sound or meaning, but for me it often seems more appropriate than "banal" or "fatuous," for example when describing much of the contents of my major hometown newspaper as well as certain prelates, politicians, and writers and/or their words.

I am in love with the word "river," both for

what it describes and simply for the way it sounds. The same goes for "nostalgia."

If I am permitted two more, I designate "audi-alnasalornithectomy," which was coined by a dear friend, the late John Slate, to describe a surgical operation for the removal, through the ear, of a bird that has flown into the patient's head through the nose. And "randle" is "a non-sensical poem recited by Irish schoolboys as an apology for farting at a friend." Truly.

Elaine Marks

(Germaine Brée Professor of French and Women's Studies, University of Wisconsin, Madison; president, Modern Language Association)

After receiving your letter, I immediately began to have a rush of words. Here are some of them and some comments about them:

Precious, luxurious, tedious, voluptuous, gorgeous, fabulous, fractious, serendipitous, posthumous, joyous, polymorphous, ubiquitous. Of course, I noticed immediately that they all end in *ous*, and that this suffix which is the ending of many adjectives means: "full of: abounding in: having: possessing the qualities of" (Webster's).

The very first word that came to mind was

"portmanteau" as in "a portmanteau word."
Again, it is an adjective, proposing a blend, or a
"combining of more than one use or quality"
(Webster's). Undoubtedly, the French connec-
tion plays a role in my pleasure, but also, like the
adjectives that end in *ous*, beyond what delights
the ear and the eye, beyond the signifier, the sig-
nified proposes richness, abundance, fullness. It
is precisely that richness, abundance, and fullness that words, representing as they do a central
absence, make present.

Peter Martins

(Ballet master in chief, New York City Ballet)

My favorite word is "stunning" because it applies
so appropriately to my world.

Bobbie Ann Mason

(Author, Spence & Lila; Feather Crowns)

My favorite word: "gigglesome."
Familiar words like "lonesome," "handsome,"
and "adventuresome" are from a whole family of
words that include some surprises that have

fallen into disuse. I heard Red Barber one morning on the radio say the air was "chillsome." Others are "grievesome," "toilsome," and "boresome." My favorites of these old words are "gigglesome" and "playsome," both usually applied to high-spirited children.

Dina Merrill
(Actress, Desk Set; The Sundowners)

My favorite swearword is "rats." I don't like to use four-letter words (except this one!) in polite company or in front of my kids, so "rats" works well for me. I seem to remember my father using it the same way when I was kid.

Ricardo Montalban
(Actor, Fantasy Island; The Wrath of Khan)

My favorite word, for obvious reasons is: "love."
  Phonetically, I like: "consuetudinary."
  Descriptively I like: "adumbrate."

David Morrell

(Author; First Blood; The Fifth Profession;
creator of the character Rambo)

My favorite words are those with which every
story I tell begins in my mind. I never fail to experience a rush of emotion as they occur to me.
Optimistic and uniquely human, they express
our capacity for wonder, our ability to create. I'll
be walking down a street or sitting at my kitchen
table, watching a movie or reading a newspaper,
and the words suddenly come unbidden to me.
"What if?" a voice inside me announces. "Suppose A did B. Suppose this happened to C. Suppose D didn't know about E and . . . Yes. What
if?" Through the alchemy of those two words,
something new comes into the world.

Desmond Morris

(Zoologist, author, The Naked Ape*)*

"Xoloitzcuintli"—the Mexican hairless dog. A small domestic dog specially bred by the Pre-Columbian Indians for use as a bed heater or "hot water bottle" to keep them warm at night. Its lack of hair gave it a skin of high temperature.

The word is a favorite of mine for the simple reason that I can pronounce it correctly (Shol-low-its-quint-lee).

"Remarkable" is a wonderful word to use when faced with something which you do not like, but which politeness prevents you from criticizing. When Winston Churchill was shown a portrait of himself by the modern artist Graham Sutherland, he described it, in his acceptance speech, as "a remarkable example of modern art." He later had it secretly burned.

"Neophilia," meaning "the love of the new." I introduced this word in the 1960s to contrast with the already commonly used "neophobia," meaning "fear of the new." Being unusually neophilic myself, I am delighted to see that it has now found its way into the latest edition of the Oxford English Dictionary.

Frederic Morton

(Author, The Rothschilds; Thunder at Twilight)

My favorite word is "cleave." It means "to adhere to firmly and closely." It also means "to divide by a cutting blow." (Definitions from the current Webster's Collegiate Dictionary.) The word haunts me because it reflects the paradox to which we life-hungry mortals are born.

Jerome T. Murphy

(Professor and dean, Harvard University Graduate School of Education)

"Zest" is a favorite word of mine. I treasure people who keenly enjoy living, those vital souls with a zest for life. Like a lemon peel in a drink, they conquer dullness and add zip.

Cleave

Wayne Myers

(Psychoanalyst, author, Shrink Dreams)

1. "Oneiric"—which translates as "dreamlike" or as "belonging to dreams" and which relates to my fascination with dreams themselves and to the unconscious forces which propel these wonderful products to the surface.

2. "Ontogeny"—which relates to the origin and development of the individual being. I especially love the use of this word in the famous scientific phrase "Ontogeny recapitulates phylogeny," which essentially means that the embryological development of the individual basically imitates the stages of the development of the history of the race or species. There is something quite magical about this concept to me.

3. "Nascent"—referring to the act of being born or brought forth and which seems to me to symbolize the act of creation itself, another magical concept to me.

Fae Myenne Ng

(Author, Bone)

"Backdaire."

I remember a hand-painted sign on Salmon Alley in San Francisco. It read: #2-4-6 Backdaire. I liked the visually translated look, the brushstroked Chinese look of the English letters—knobby and inky at the tops and bottoms, lean through the middle. Probably written by an oldtimer who spoke English when only absolutely necessary. I liked that the careful spelling (maybe inspired by Frigidaire?) captured his accent. I love how this word captured the ingenuity of the oldtimer's spirit and also something of his mischievous brand of courage: What you don't know, just make up.

Sometime in 1990 the building was painted and the word was not rewritten on the wall. For me the word "backdaire" is like a foundation. Like the home in China I've always heard referred to as "back there," and the better times as "back then," the written word "backdaire" claims my place here and addresses my home now.

Joyce Carol Oates

(Novelist, poet, Them, Bellefleur, Foxfire)

"Phantasmajoria." "Chiaroscuro." "Palimpsest." "Intransigent."

Why are these among my favorite words? I think because of their sounds as well as their meanings; and their hidden meanings, for me as a writer, as well as their explicit, dictionary meanings. They suggest depths and dimensions of mystery.

Douglas O'Brien

(New York broadcaster, Dialogue)

My favorite word:

"Jerzoid"—a delightful pejorative of my wife's invention, I think. At least I first heard it from her when she screamed it at a cab driver with New Jersey plates who nearly ran her down at a Manhattan street corner. Jerzoids are universally despised by English-speaking New York City cab drivers. Only non-English-speaking New York City cab drivers enjoy lower status. The appellation has also come to mean a dolt of any origin.

Sidney Offit

(Television personality, author,
The Adventures of Homer Fink)

I fell in love with the word "chimera" when I was fifteen years old and the managing editor of the student newspaper of the Valley Forge Military Academy. I was desperately in need of a vocabulary to distinguish my editorials from the hut-two-three-four compositions of senior cadets. "Chimera" was everything I thought a word should be—and more. It had classical derivations: "she goat" from the Greek and "a fire-breathing monster with the head of a lion, the body of a goat, and the tail of a serpent" from the Latin. The contemporary usage was defined as "a creation of the imagination: an impossible and foolish fancy."

I never said the word because I was unsure of how to pronounce it; but I exploited the ace of my vocabulary in print frequently, recklessly. I anointed Chamberlain's "peace in our time," the Maginot line, and character-building sessions of the academy's commandant as chimeras. By the winter of 1948 I expressed my frustration with the Henry Wallace presidential campaign in the editorial pages of the campus newspaper of the Johns Hopkins University by dubbing the Progressive Party candidate a "chimera."

Later, my favorite word provided the inspiration for a novel for young readers, *The Adventures of Homer Fink*. It is the story of a Baltimore schoolboy who believes in Greek deities. For several decades *Homer* appeared in various editions and sold briskly. I was beginning to believe I had achieved the writer's dream: a minor classic. Several years ago *Homer* went out of print. My illusions of literary immortality were "a foolish fancy"—a chimera.

Ben Okri

(Booker Prize–winning author, The Famished Road; Songs of Enchantment)

My favorite word of the moment is "illumination."

Frank Oz

(One of the creators of the Muppets; voice of Bert, Grover, and others)

I don't have a favorite word (however, if I did, "Frumkes" would be right there at the top of the list—if you allow names to be words). One word does strike me as most interesting, though. It is "onomatopoeia." I think I like it because it sounds so much like what it is.

Cynthia Ozick

(Author, The Shawl; Cannibal Galaxy)

"Pellucid," because of both the (limpid, lucent) sound and the nearly utopian slant of meaning. An intensity of clarity—of light, of openness, of truth, of person, of history. "Pellucid" suggests—or promises—that nothing more than the thinnest, most transparent membrane lies between longing and enlightenment.

Abraham Pais

(Physicist, friend and biographer of Albert Einstein)

The choice is hard. But one of my life's mottoes is:

> "The situation is impossible, but not hopeless."

Linus Pauling

(Scientist, Nobel prizes in chemistry and peace)

I feel strongly about the expression "peace and friendship," for obvious reasons.

There are also a number of words used by physicists and chemists that appeal to me, but would not appeal to the public in general. I shall accordingly say that my favorite word is "parallelepiped." It is pronounced parallel-epi-ped. *Epi* means "around" and *ped* means "faces." A rectangular parallelepiped has six faces perpendicular to each other, each face being a rectangle. Many people write the word as "parallelopiped," and pronounce it parallel-o-pi-ped. This spelling and pronunciation are wrong.

I remember that about sixty years ago I used the word "parallelepiped" in my lecture, and one of my brightest students jumped suddenly, indicating to me that he was astonished. I think that he decided that finally he had caught me making a mistake.

David Pearce

(Ophthalmologist, student of the American language)

I'm particularly enthralled and enamored by words that have their own euphony—words that go trippingly off the tongue: "inexorable," "felicitous," "impugn," "ineffable," and "ineluctable," to cite a few.

David Pearson

(President Pearson-McGuire, Public Relations, Coral Gables, Florida)

My favorite word is "insufferable!" Once in an old movie I saw a French nobleman being insulted by a drunken English actor backstage in a theater, while the nobleman was waiting for an actress, with whom they were both smitten, to dress. First the nobleman said, sotto voce to himself, "Disgusting!" Then a few seconds later, as the drunk continued to make fun of the snooty noble, he muttered "Outrageous!" But the final word, which he hurled at both the actress, who was stifling a smile, and the drunk, vastly enjoying his discomfort, was "Insufferable!" And with that word, he flung his cape over his shoulder and fled the dressing room.

This, you see, is a much more expressive epithet than, say, "Shut up!" or even "I say!" if you happen to be of noble birth.

Arno Penzias

(Nobel laureate in physics, 1978)

My favorite word is "affidavit."

The first English word I ever learned—Germany, 1938.

As a Jewish child in Nazi Germany, I heard the grown-ups talking about this evidently wonderful thing they all wanted. Fortunately, my family got one at the last minute and we were able to come to America.

Regina Peruggi

(President, Marymount Manhattan College)

Picking out favorite words is like asking me to pick out favorite students—I love them all and each one for a different reason. But here are three words that I like, all for very different reasons.

The first word is "unconscionable." Though I rarely use it when I write, I love to say it, for its sound seems to resonate its meaning. So, when I'm absolutely aghast, shocked, or overwhelmed with the injustice of it all, "unconscionable" always seems the most fitting way to express my sentiments.

The second word I've chosen is as soft in sound to me as the first is harsh. That word is "cherish." I like it better than almost any other term of endearment, for the word "cherish" epitomizes for me the feeling of keeping something or someone at the very deepest spot of my heart.

Finally, growing up in the Bronx, I had certain words that I would call part of our very own vocabulary. We drank "egg creams," played "potsy," went to the movies at the Lo-wees (Loews) Paradise, and knew that "irregardless" of what other people said about us, people from the Bronx were the best. Somehow, "irregardless" of my schooling, I've never let it interfere with my education in the Bronx!!!

147

●◇ ●◇ ●◇

Steven Pinker

(Professor, Department of Brain and Cognitive Sciences, MIT; author, The Language Instinct)

I like the irregular verbs of English, all 180 of them, because of what they tell us about the history of the language and the human minds that have perpetuated it.

The irregulars are defiantly quirky. Thousands of verbs monotonously take the *-ed* suffix for their past tense forms, but *ring* mutates to *rang*, not *ringed*, *catch* becomes *caught*, *hit* doesn't do anything, and *go* is replaced by an entirely different word, *went* (a usurping of the old past tense of *to wend;* which itself once followed the pattern we see in *send-sent* and *bend-bent).* No wonder irregular verbs are banned in "rationally designed" languages like Esperanto and Orwell's Newspeak—and why recently a woman in search of a nonconformist soul-mate wrote a personal ad that began, "Are you an irregular verb?"

Since irregulars are unpredictable, people can't derive them on the fly as they talk, but have to have memorized them beforehand one by one, just like simple unconjugated words, which are also unpredictable. (The word *duck* does not look like a duck, walk like a duck, or quack like a duck.) Indeed, the irregulars are all good, basic English words: Anglo-Saxon monosyllables. (The seeming exceptions are just monosyllables disguised by a prefix: *became* is *be-* + *came; understood* is *under-* + *stood; forgot* is *for-* + *got*).

There are tantalizing patterns among the irregulars: *ring-rang, sing-sang, spring-sprang, drink-drank, shrink-shrank, sink-sank, stink-stank; blow-blew, grow-grew, know-knew, throw-threw, draw-drew, fly-flew, slay-slew; swear-swore, wear-wore, bear-bore, tear-tore.* But they still resist being captured by a rule. Next to *sing-sang* we find not *cling-clang* but *cling-clung,* not *think-thank* but *think-thought,* not *blink-blank* but *blink-blinked.* In between *blow-blew* and *grow-grew* sits *glow-glowed. Wear-wore* may inspire *swear-swore,* but *tear-tore* does not inspire *stare-store.* This chaos is a legacy of the Indo-Europeans, the remarkable prehistoric tribe whose language took over most of Europe and southwestern Asia. Their language formed tenses using rules that regularly replaced one vowel with another. But as pronunciation habits changed in their descendant tribes, the rules became opaque to children and eventually died; the irregular past tense forms are their fossils. So every time we use an irregular verb, we are continuing a game of Broken Telephone that has gone on for more than five thousand years.

I especially like the way that irregular verbs graciously relinquish their past tense forms in special circumstances, giving rise to a set of quirks that have puzzled language mavens for decades but which follow an elegant principle that every speaker of the language—every jock, every four-year-old—tacitly knows. In baseball, one says that a slugger has *flied out;* no mere mortal has ever "flown out" to center field. When the designated goon on a hockey team is sent to the penalty box for nearly decapitating the opposing team's finesse player, he has *high-sticked,* not *high-stuck.* Ross Perot has *grandstanded,* but he has never *grandstood,* and the Serbs have *ringed* Sarajevo with artillery, but have never *rung* it. What these suddenly regular verbs have in common is that they are based on nouns: to hit a fly that gets caught, to clobber with a high stick, to play to the grandstand, to form a ring around. These are verbs with noun roots, and a noun cannot have an irregular past tense connected to it because a noun cannot have a past tense at all—what would it mean for a hockey stick to have a past tense? So the irregular form is sealed off and the regular "add -*ed*" rule fills the vacuum. One of the wonderful features about this law is that it belies the accusations of self-appointed guardians of the language that modern speakers are slowly eroding the noun-verb distinction by cavalierly turning nouns into verbs *(to parent, to input, to impact,* and so on). Verbing nouns makes the language more sophisticated, not less so: people use different kinds of past tense forms for plain old verbs and verbs based on nouns, so they must be keeping track of the difference between the two.

Do irregular verbs have a future? At first glance, the prospects do not seem good. Old English had more than twice as many irregular verbs as we do today. As some of the verbs became less common, like *cleave-clove, abide-abode,* and *geld-gelt,* children failed to memorize their irregular forms and applied the *-ed* rule instead (just as today children are apt to say *winded* and *speaked*). The irregular forms were doomed for these children's children and for all subsequent generations (though some of the dead irregulars have left souvenirs among the English adjectives, like *cloven, cleft, shod, gilt,* and *pent*).

Not only is the irregular class losing members by emigration, it is not gaining new ones by immigration. When new verbs enter English via onomatopoeia *(to ding, to ping),* borrowings from other languages *(deride* and *succumb* from Latin), and conversions from nouns *(fly out),* the regular rule has first dibs on them. The language ends up with *dinged, pinged, derided, succumbed,* and *flied out,* not *dang, pang, derode, succame,* or *flew out.*

But many of the irregulars can sleep securely, for they have two things on their side. One is their sheer frequency in the language. The ten commonest verbs in English *(be, have, do, say, make, go, take, come, see,* and *get)* are all irregular, and about 70 percent of the time we use a verb, it is an irregular verb. And children have a wondrous capacity for memorizing words; they pick up a new one every two hours, accumulating 60,000 by high school. Eighty irregulars are common enough that children use them before they learn to read, and I predict they will stay in the language indefinitely.

And there is one small opportunity for growth. Irregulars have to be memorized, but human memory distills out any pattern it can find in the memorized items. People occasionally apply a pattern to a new verb in an attempt to be cool, funny, or distinctive. Dizzy Dean *slood* into second base; a Boston eatery once sold T-shirts that read "I got *schrod* at Legal Seafood," and many people occasionally report that they *snoze, squoze, shat,* or *have tooken* something. Could such forms ever catch on and become standard? Perhaps. A century ago, some creative speaker must have been impressed by the pattern in *stick-stuck* and *strike-struck,* and that is how our youngest irregular, *snuck,* sneaked in.

George Plimpton

(Author, Paper Lion; Mad Ducks and Bears;
editor-in-chief, The Paris Review)

"Wimbledon."

"Wimbledon" is my favorite word, especially
when the tournament is held there and I imagine
myself getting at least to the semifinals.

Letty Cottin Pogrebin

(Feminist, author, Among Friends)

My favorite word is "onomatopoeia," which defines the use of words whose sound communi-
cates or suggests their meanings. "Babble,"
"hiss," "tickle," and "buzz" are examples of onomatopoeic usage.

The word "onomatopoeia" charms me because
of its pleasing sound and symbolic precision. I
love its lilting alternation of consonant and
vowel, its tongue-twisting syllabic complexity, its
playfulness. Those who do not know its meaning
might guess it to be the name of a creeping ivy,
or a bacterial infection, or maybe a small village
in Sicily. But those acquainted with the word understand that it, too, in some quirky way, embodies its meaning.

153

"Onomatopoeia" is a writer's word and a reader's nightmare but the language would be poorer without it.

Roman Polanski
(Film director, Chinatown; Repulsion;
Bitter Moon)

One of my favorite words is *kurwa*! A dirty Polish word meaning "whore." A favorite swearword of my compatriots.

Reynolds Price
(Author, Blue Calhoun; Kate Vaiden)

I know that my favorite words in childhood were two—"Reynolds Price." By the time I was five or six, I'd get off alone and repeat them tonelessly until they became a kind of protective spell. Was I preparing myself for a lifetime of pernicious narcissism, or was I just unearthing the normal born-writer's obsession with words for their own sake? I vote for the latter.

Since then I've been aware of certain words that tend to recur in my writing, but I can't say that their use gives me unusual shivers of pleasure. Take a single example—the word "dense." I'm always having to weed its excess appearances out of manuscripts and proofs; and aside from the fact that I may just be a congenitally dense human being, I can't honestly guess why the word insists on volunteering in my work.

Come to think of it, though, it's a worthy syllable—dense itself in sound and brevity and as elegant in its homely pressed-down compactness as I've always wanted my speech and life to be.

W. V. Quine

(Edgar Pierce Professor of Philosophy Emeritus, Harvard University, author of twenty books)

I am pleased and flattered by your invitation to celebrate my favorite words. I hate some words, mostly latter-day coinages that gratuitously mix Latin and Greek. On the other hand, I am at a loss for favorites. Donald Davidson once told me that I overdo "actually," but I have been unaware of any particular fondness for it. If I have reacted by using it more than ever, it has been in a spirit rather of self-mockery or bravado.

Maxwell M. Rabb

(Ambassador to Italy during Reagan Administration)

The noun "delegate" is my favorite word, for it has changed the course of my life three times. First, I was a delegate to the Massachusetts State Convention the year that it nominated Henry Cabot Lodge, Jr., to be its candidate to the United States Senate. He won, and I went to Washington as his administrative assistant.

Second, I was a delegate to the convention that nominated Dwight D. Eisenhower to be its candidate for the presidency. He won, and I went to the White House as his special assistant and secretary to the Cabinet.

Finally, I was a delegate to the Republican National Convention that nominated Ronald Reagan. He won, and I went to Italy as the American ambassador, where I served for eight years. "Delegate" is my favorite word. For me, it means more than just a political office; it also conveys a sense of hope and opportunity.

Dan Rather

(CBS TV News anchorman)

My two favorite words carry strong associations with my parents. When you think about it, they were the first people to teach me the use of language, so I guess it stands to reason that my favorite words remind me of them.

My father's word was "courage," a word that meant a lot to him beyond the dictionary meaning: coming from his mouth it was a one-word pep talk in tough times. A fine old word—"take heart"—and a benediction I continue to invoke (but no longer on the *CBS Evening News*). My father tried all his life to give his children the things we'd need, not just dinner on the table but tools for the future. Courage—the word *and* the spirit—he gave us aplenty. On my best days, I hope I'm worthy of my father's legacy, at least a little.

In the neighborhood where I grew up, there was a field or vacant lot that my mother always called a "meadow." It was the most beautiful word she knew. Mother was strong and gentle, and "meadow" has a strong and gentle sound: the stretch of the short *e* and the long *o* clipped off. For my mother, the word conjured images of sunshine and peace, of nature that didn't threaten even if it wasn't altogether tamed. Those images fit my mother, too.

Lynn Redgrave

(Actress, Georgie Girl)

"Jibber."

Used in our household as a word to describe any kind of remote control device (TV–video–garage door–gate opener).

We don't know how we came to use this word–but strangely, not only our children but stray visitors and acquaintances seem to know exactly what we are talking about.

Even my eighty-three-year-old mother in England now knows what a "jibber" is.

"Jibber," what a satisfying word!

Leni Riefenstahl

(German filmmaker/photographer, Triumph of the Will; Olympiad)

My favorite word is "passion" because "passion" is the root of all creative work.

Passion

Mandy Riner

(Student in the author's honors Critical Thinking class at Marymount Manhattan College)

Just since I've moved to New York City has "y'all" become my favorite word. Back home in Georgia, "y'all" is as common as bagel shops are in New York City. "Y'all" is a kind of symbol of where I'm from. It is a southern word, and because of that, I say it with great pride. The word is also very contagious. I keep catching many of the friends I have made up here saying "y'all" and then either laughing at themselves or cursing me. Another reason I like "y'all" so much is that it can be used in just about any context. It can be a greeting, an expression of disgust, a summoning, or just about anything that has to do with talking to and with a group of people.

Joan Rivers

(Comedienne, actress)

I like "cellar door." It's the most beautiful-sounding word in the English language. If you say it as one word, it is *sooooooo* pretty.

P.S. My second favorite word is "money" and my third and fourth together are "rich person."

A. M. Rosenthal

(Columnist and former editor,
The New York Times)

PRESIDENT to SECRETARY OF STATE: "Who thought up this Bosnia plan?"

SECRETARY: "I did, sir."

PRESIDENT: "Well, I've seen some ridiculous plans, but you can bet your sweet patootie this one is really cockamamie."

Jack Rosenthal

(Editor, The New York Times Magazine)

Let me cast my lot with the word "palmetto." It became a metaphoric favorite about ten years ago when my son John came home from high school with a vocabulary list whose words he declared to be "stupid and useless." What with SATs drawing near, I inspected the list and pronounced the stupid and useless words to be inspiring. "Well, no one ever actually uses those words," John insisted. "You would never use them in *The Times.*"

You know what happened next. I took the list

of words and, during the course of the next week, worked all twenty into one or another editorial. Words like "alabaster" and "antiquity" were easy; the hardest, as you've already divined, was "palmetto," but I finally got that in, too.

Only to be immediately deflated. At home that night, John had a new list. "These are even dumber words," he said. So I worked all twenty new words into editorials the following week. And then, the week after that, came parents' visiting day. I couldn't resist rushing up to Susan Sherman, the English teacher, to describe my exertions in support of her vocabulary lessons. Her response was startling. "Why, that little sneak!" she said with an unfolding grin. Sneak? Yes. The pupils were meant not only to learn the words. They had been instructed to find them in *print.*

So when you ask for my favorite word, I have 500 to choose from, since I ended up getting the whole term's list onto the editorial page—"timorous" and "truculent," "cantata" and "cantilever," "attenuate" and "reverberate." But one word stands tall: "palmetto," gracefully fanning the air and marking the maturing of a son who had his father's number.

Henry Rosovsky

*(Lewis P. and Linda L. Geyser University Professor
of Economics, Former Dean of Arts and Sciences,
Harvard University; principal architect
of the core curriculum)*

I am enclosing a copy of my favorite words and they are the quote from Master William Johnson Cory of Eaton as cited in my book *The University: An Owner's Manual.*

You are not engaged so much in acquiring knowledge as in making mental efforts under criticism. A certain amount of knowledge you can indeed with average faculties acquire so as to retain; nor need you regret the hours that you have spent on much that is forgotten, for the shadow of lost knowledge at least protects you from many illusions.

But you go to a great school, not for knowledge so much as for arts and habits; for the habit of attention, for the art of expression, for the art of assuming at a moment's notice a new intellectual posture, for the art of entering quickly into another person's thoughts, for the habit of submitting to censure and refutation, for the art of indicating assent or dissent in graduated terms, for the habit of regarding minute points of accuracy, for the habit of working out what is possible in a given time, for taste, for discrimination, for mental courage and mental soberness.

Above all, you go to a great school for self-knowledge.

I love these words because they are the best description of a liberal education that I have ever found.

Wilbur Ross
(Banker, CEO, Rothschild Inc.)

"More" was the theme song of that great movie *Mondo Cane* and of my first wedding. The marriage failed so I dropped the song but found another use for the word. Now, in every corporate restructuring, I say over and over and over, "more, more, more," until the proponents of "less" give up.

After years of living with "more," I began to understand how important it is to everything we do. "More" is the issue between management and labor, landlord and tenant, parent and child, husband and wife, politician and taxpayer, addict and pusher. Americans who say "More" more than 100 times per day are much more likely to become richer and have better sex lives than

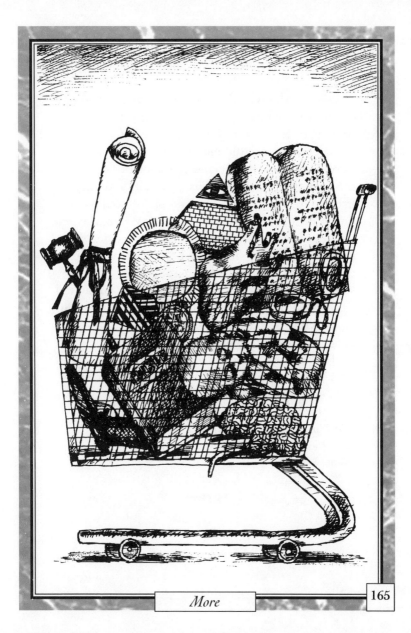

those who do not. "More" also was the Yuppie buzzword.

Despite the word's significance, the etymology of "more" is unclear. Some reputable scholars trace it to the pagan god of plenty, Erom, which a dyslectic translator made into "more." Equally unreliable sources ascribe the root of "more" to the archaic Latin "moreleisa," which was the approximate weight an average slave could carry one mile up a 10 percent grade. When slavery ended, the newly liberated Italian workers absconded with the "lessa," whom they worship to this day, leaving more for management. My personal favorite theory is that the word emanated from the Plattdeutsch *Muchen moren moster,* a superlative originally applied to outstanding lager beer. As chemists replaced Meisterbrewers, quality fell and the word dissolved. First *Muchen* and later *mosten,* leaving only *moren.* During the German exodus to America a century ago, the *n* was left on the dock at Bremerhaven. Only "more" made it across the Atlantic.

Wherever it came from, "more" is better, so go for it. I have.

Howard Rubenstein

(CEO, Howard J. Rubenstein Associates)

My list of favorite words includes:

"Monster"—Denoting an enormous achievement that is felt throughout the City of New York.

"Mediate and negotiate"—In a city that is as diverse as New York, these two actions are among the most important efforts business, community, and government leaders can participate in.

"Pride"—This word is defined as being a New Yorker. We take pride in being the nosiest, the most creative, the brashest, and yes, even the rudest if that's what it takes to get the job done.

"Schlep"—Yiddish in origin. Anyone who works on Seventh Avenue uses this word with the ease of their native tongue to describe what they have been doing all day.

"Excel"—The standard of competition in a very demanding environment. As you linger on the word, you can almost hear the tires screech away from the competition.

"Ethical"—The moral compass by which to steer professional and personal behavior.

"So?"—For all intents and purposes, a greeting but reflective of the Jewish tradition of asking "why" even when there isn't a question on the table.

"Novel"—in a world that bores easily, creating something novel and creative still generates respect.

"Great!"—The word remains one of the simplest yet most effective exclamations in our vocabulary. You rarely see anyone exclaim, "Mediocre!" It is "Great!" that commands respect.

Edward Said

(Literary critic, author; The World, the Text, & the Critic; Orientalism; Culture & Imperialism)

There are a group of words beginning with the letter *v* that hold a particular pleasure for me. This is only partially connected with their meaning. Words like "virtuoso" and "virtuosity," "voluptuous," "volatile," "vivacity," "vortex," "vertiginous" (or "vertigo," which I find less interesting) and "victorious" (more so than "victory," which seems curiously abstract and a bit disdainful). All these *v* words communicate something exceptional and quite out of the ordinary, a sensation of the extra, the brilliant, even the dangerous, and also lots of, well, "vitality." I have realized that I use them in my own writing as a kind of special reward for what I'm trying to say, words not pronounced lightly or immediately but bestowed on an experience or person at the end and after trying in many other words to put my finger on something quite unique. Looking recently at a videotape of Glenn Gould playing an extract on the piano from Strauss's *Elektra*—reducing the mammoth orchestral score to a brilliantly complex keyboard version, conducting it with a free hand here, singing the parts of Elektra and her sister Chrysosthemis in German there, his face transfigured by the rich complexity of what was going on, his incredibly agile and expressive fingers flawlessly negotiating the music with such inevitability and mastery—and the word "virtuosity" was pulled out of me as if from my unconscious.

My own language, Arabic, doesn't have a *v*, so that there's an additional pleasure in the rare novelty of these words, quite unique to English.

Sebastiao Salgado

(Award-winning Brazilian photographer, Workers: The Archaeology of the Industrial Age)

My favorite word is *travessia,* a Portuguese word meaning our movement. We came from one place and we go to another. We are in *travessia,* in movement, in transition, in passing.

Harrison Salisbury

(Pulitzer Prize–winning author, The Nine Hundred Days: The Siege of Leningrad)

My favorite word is "pumpkin." I don't know why. But "pumpkin" touches off some childhood habits of mine. You can't take it seriously. But you can't ignore it either. It takes ahold of your head and that's it. You are a pumpkin. Or you are not. I am.

Abbie Salny

(Supervisory psychologist, Mensa; author, Mensa
Genius Quiz Books; *co-author, with Lewis
Frumkes,* Mensa Think Smart Book)

As far as I am concerned, my favorite word is "pommard." It rolls mellifluously off the tongue, conjuring up visions of its actual self rolling equally smoothly and deliciously down the tongue and then the throat. It reverberates with sunlight, green leaves, and deep purple. It echoes in the caverns of memory with the remembered olfactory and gustatory pleasures. If pronounced in French, as it should be, it has a roll and a resonance that truly reflects its noble origin.

My second most favorite word is "facetiously." Not only does it have all the vowels in proper sequence, thus providing me with a quiz question when I am asked for one in a hurry, it sounds like what it is. It has a humorous and amusing tone; when pronounced, it brings up visions of comedy, humor, and a light sort of wit that I savor. It is semi-erudite, thus pleasing my vocabulary-oriented tastes, but is well recognized and can be used appropriately in almost any company.

●◇ ●◇ ●◇

Stephen Sandy

(Poet, Man in the Open Air;
Thanksgiving over the Water)

"Qualmish." Having a feeling of fear, misgiving, or depression. Excellent word when asked how one feels on Monday morning; i.e., fine to use as alternative for the preemptive *kvetch*—instead of "don't ask." Also has the ring and effect of an indigenous tribe that lived on cranberries, oysters, and quail. "Oh, yes, the Qualmish, they used to banquet on the shores of this river. The middens of their shells are not infrequent among the rushes."

"Scatheless." A hard Scandinavian opening—with an aural effect like "scald" or "scrape" or "scull"—but with a lovely finish, a mellow diminuendo with the voiced *th* and the lingering *l* and dying *s*'s; the first syllable like a spike of vodka; the second, a swallow of venerable Richebourg. And of course it describes that most enviable of conditions: the *unharmed*—nay, more; the word denotes rather the state of being not-get-at-able; not of merely escaping harm, but of *being* off the hook, *being* far from harm's way.

"Pergola." I love this word for its evocation of a time of seeming grace, of sunlit leisure on spacious American afternoons. When I used the word in a class some years ago, a student (he was from the big city) had never heard of a pergola, and asked what one was; the denotative meaning was simple enough, yet he could not get why the word had such an aura for me, so to suggest its connotations, I wrote a poem to explain one word:

The macadam is flaking and the lilac
Too big to bloom
Fingers a cobweb of smoky light from the
    terrace,
Grazes the sun-chalked cedarshakes. And no
    surprise.

Gone the lady to Athens or Anjou. Her sunroom
Oozes silence. The paisley over the back
Of a wicker rocker. The pedals of her grand
    hover
Above the calm sea of the tiled floor.

Like gilt clouds, each brazen ball
Without a claw. In Roseville jardinieres
Iron geraniums stiffen and chip;
A noose of rose and the scum of ferrous

Oxide throttle the sundial's Horatian tip
For those noddy panamas and white-ducks of
    class.
In the pergola woodflies on the pedestal
Walk all over it. What are years?

Or at the stoned gazing globe's crashed glass
Peek in on themselves, magnified; what's more,
Behold no Chloe or her golfing lover
In the mullioned saucers of their eyes.

Francesco Scavullo
(Fashion photographer)

My favorite word: "Shittheworldisfullofit."
   That's one word.

George Schindler
(Magician)

Saying the magical words "Ah Choleria," one can
cause objects to float, flowers to appear and disappear, and tigers to change places with people.
One can do this if he or she is also a magician.
Fortunately, I am, and the words "Ah Choleria"
are the words I chose to replace the tired old
"abracadabra."

Before using the words, remember that there
must be a small pause between them. The *ch*
sound is pronounced gutturally, as in the German *achtung,* or like the *ch* in *chutzpah.*

Literally translated from the Yiddish, it means
"a cholera" and was used with other words in the
context of a mild curse. "May a cholera take
you!" or as a substitute for "damn it" when something has gone wrong. You curse the happening

174

rather than any person. Another application is to describe an event as "terrible." (Example: "How was the movie?" Reply: "Ah Choleria.")

In my act, when I want the magic to happen, I announce, "Saying the magic words, Ah Choleria . . ." just before the denouement. When the laugh comes, I follow with, "I see a few of my people are in the room tonight."

A few years ago during a performance in Christchurch, New Zealand, I used the phrase as usual. A single laugh came from the rear of the theater. After the show a gentleman came forward and introduced himself. "I am one of the six Jews in Christchurch."

Try the words at your next party. (There must be some potential for the word "Frumkes.")

Mary Schmidt-Campbell
(Dean, Tisch School of the Arts, New York University)

My word is "ineluctable."

Steven Schragis

(Publisher, Carol Publishing Group)

My word actually isn't an English word—it's French.

When I was about twelve years old, I took a trip with my family to various cities in Europe. My parents' stated purpose was to teach their children something about European culture and style, and though I don't think they accomplished that goal, we did have a good time.

At a fancy hotel in Paris, my sister came across the word *pamplemousse* in the breakfast section of the room service menu. We were intrigued by this word, and so the following morning called to order some. The room service operator spoke just a bit of English, and innocently inquired whether we wanted *pamplemousse* or *pamplemousse* juice! For some reason my sister thought this was the funniest thing she ever heard and began laughing so hard, she could not continue her conversation. I was in no better shape, and as only an obnoxious twelve-year-old can do, I slammed down the telephone.

About twenty minutes later two sliced grapefruits arrived at the room, as did two glasses of grapefruit juice. As grapefruits were imported into France from abroad, the bill for all of this was nearly 350 francs—at that time over 50 dollars. This was not at all funny to my parents, who don't remember the whole incident in a particularly humorous light.

To this day, even though we both prefer orange juice to grapefruit juice, my sister and I order *"pamplemousse* juice" in restaurants because we love the word so much.

Robert Schuller

(TV evangelist, Crystal Cathedral Ministries)

My two favorite words: "Wow!" and "Hallelujah!"

Glenn Seaborg

(Nobel Prize in chemistry, 1951; former chairman, Atomic Energy Commission)

I have had a number of favorite words that I used especially when our six children were growing up. One of these was "kumquat"; I recall saying "kumquat may" (come what may) and that I wanted for dinner "kumquats and fried rainwater." One of my favorite alliterations was to "derogate, denigrate, deprecate, deride, and decry"; my kids, in later years, claim I was trying to

177

increase their vocabulary, and perhaps they were right. When they were small, I used to threaten, when they were naughty, that I would "impy-do" them or even "roog" them (pronounced like "root" with a hard *g*); I guess I liked the sound of these contrived words. I often say that I am doing something with "impunity"; my wife, Helen, avers that I am referring to a lady friend with the name "impunity." My administrative assistant claims I favor the words "perspicacious" and "perspicuous" and I do admit to liking their sound. Another favorite word is "alacrity" (let's move with alacrity).

Wilfrid Sheed

(Novelist, essayist, critic, The Morning After; Max Jamison)

I'm too much of a whore, or philandering philologist, or whatever, to have a favorite word. As soon as I take a shine to one, I realize I've probably been using it too much and it has to go back to the end of the line. So my favorite word is always the one I haven't used lately but which fills the bill perfectly. In the last year or so, I believe I got off a pretty good "plangent" (I wouldn't touch "lambent" with a ten-foot pole) and adequate "ragamuffin," and for the late William Shawn, my first and last "fussbudget"—though don't hold me to this; it might come in handy again if I ever have to write about Ross Perot or Robert Dole.

But there have been hundreds of favorite words over the years that have nothing to recommend them but aptness: they fit the hole in the puzzle, and you have to love a word that does that, even if it's one you wouldn't look at on another occasion. For instance, the word "aptness"; plain as an old shoe, but it gets you from here to there when the "multitudinous seas incarnadine" aren't running. And you can use it twice, because nobody saw it the first time.

Cybill Shepherd

(Actress: television, Moonlighting; *film,* The Last Picture Show)

"Ubiquitous."

Jane Smiley

(Pulitzer Prize–winning author,
A Thousand Acres)

My favorite words are all fairly obvious — "garlicky," which is exactly how I like everything I eat. Here's a good recipe: Peel 16 cloves of garlic and rub a little salt and paprika on the pieces of a cut-up 3-pound chicken. Pour a little olive oil into a sauté pan, and toast a 5-inch-long slice of French bread until it is golden on both sides. Take out the bread, and put in the garlic and chicken. Brown them together over medium heat for 15 minutes, then take out the garlic and pour off the fat. Add 1/2 cup white wine and 1/2 cup water. Cook the chicken for 10 more minutes, or until cooked through. Put the garlic, the bread (cut into chunks), the juices from the pot, 1 tablespoon cognac, and 1/2 teaspoon saffron threads into a food processor and process. Add salt and pepper to taste, then reheat the sauce with the chicken. Serve with mashed potatoes. I like Yukon Golds or Rose Golds. This is a Spanish recipe from *Bon Appétit*. I have never met a recipe for chicken with garlic that I didn't like.

I like the word "baby," because the *b*'s remind me of round baby cheeks.

I like the sound of the words "Krakatoa" and "glistening." Probably the word I tend to overuse most often is "clearly," which I also like very much.

Robin Smith
(President and CEO, Publishers Clearing House)

A favorite word of mine is "callipygian" (actually I now find I was erroneously using the word, saying "callipygious" instead). Anyway, I like it because it is unusual—and I'm amazed and amused that someone went to the trouble to make up a word for "having shapely buttocks." Another one I like is "cacophony" because it really conveys its meaning—maybe I also like hard syllables.

Albert Solnit
(Sterling Professor Emeritus, Child Study Center, Yale University)

I am not aware of having a favorite word, but as I've been thinking about it, I have a favorite saying that I did not create but which I learned from a distinguished professor of pediatrics, Daniel Darrow, who died several years ago. He used to say (and I have used this over and over again), "When there's too much teaching, there's not enough learning." I have spent a good deal of my life as a teacher who learned some years ago that it is the privilege of the teacher to enable students to become active in learning about what interests them and about what they need to know to help themselves to acquire the competence they seek and the satisfaction they'll gain from being in charge of themselves.

Stephen Spahn
(Educator, headmaster, The Dwight School)

"Cockeyed," as in "this cockeyed world!"

Anytime of the day or night . . . anywhere in the world, I turn on the TV or read the newspapers and the impressions come flooding in: horrors beyond imagining, suffering, inhumanity, plagues of biblical proportions, wars and rumors of wars, ecological disasters upon disasters, crises without end. Yes, this is a cockeyed world, all right! And yet, is there not a bit of optimism lurking somewhere in the word? Does it not imply at least a smidgin of hope? Is there not, just possibly, a hint of *enthusiasm for life* in the word "cockeyed"?

I sit in my office at The Dwight School and

182

Cockeyed

turn off the TV, put away the newspaper, and watch the smiling, bubbling faces passing my door. Each child is a universe, full of almost unbounded potential . . . and each one is different. I am privileged to head a school where the individual talents of each student are identified, nourished, developed, and polished. We have created a number of special programs, such as the Dwight Sports Institute, which enables scholar-athletes to reach Olympic training levels while receiving top-quality academic instruction. A national sailing champion passes the door, as well as an Ivy League tennis captain—both products of the Institute.

Others come by: a classicist who will study Early Hittite language at Columbia; a returning graduate who is now president of his class at a prestigious law school; an ambassador's son who came to Dwight to learn about America and has himself become a great ambassador to his fellow students. The school is full of these stories.

Why do I believe in these youngsters? Will they succeed where others have fallen? Yes, I believe in them because I am a cockeyed optimist! Because as an educator, I know that if I can ignite that inner fire in each child, the torch will be carried onward. I always want to remain close enough to young people to draw on their sense of wonder and unbounded possibilities. The light in their eyes is the best antidote to the problems of this cockeyed world.

Gloria Steinem

(Feminist, author, editor, Ms. *magazine)*

My favorite word is "empathy."

Robert J. Sternberg

(IBM Professor of Psychology and Education, Yale University)

My very favorite word is *Alejandra*. That's the name of my wife, and she is incomparable: One couldn't have a better wife.

After that my favorite words are *schlemiel* and *schlimazel*. The schlemiel, as we know, is the one who spills the chicken soup on the schlimazel. The reason I like these words so much is that they capture so much of what life is about. Some people are constantly dumping on others—that is, there are schlemiels constantly dumping on schlimazels. And the words capture most of abnormal psychology as well. There are those who cause problems for others, and those who allow others to cause problems for them. We have a garden variety of fancy names for them, but we don't really understand why these people are the way they are, and it pretty much boils down to schlemiels and schlimazels again. I have a lot more to say, but people are constantly phoning me and knocking on my door and otherwise bringing me problems, and I have to attend to them, not to mention wiping the chicken soup off me. . . .

Fred Mustard Stewart
(Author, Mephisto Waltz)

My favorite word is "chthonic" (pronounced "thonic"), which means "pertaining to the gods and spirits of the underworld." It is my favorite word because I've never seen it used except once, in a *very* obscure English short story. No one has the foggiest notion what it means, and whoever saw a word start with *chth*? I'll admit it has been somewhat difficult to work it into a conversation.

Leo Stone
(Psychoanalyst)

A word that has always fascinated me is "irredentist" or "irredentism." It means "unredeemed," and comes from "Italia Irredenta," which was an organization that became prominent in the late nineteenth century for advocating the incorporation of certain neighboring regions into Italy. I use "irredentist" in a more personal way to explain people who are trying to recapture or redeem something in their lives.

Mark Strand
(Poet, The Owl's Insomnia; The Late Hour)

Abacaxi—which is Portuguese for "pineapple."
   Morbido—which is Italian for "soft."
   "Icebox."

Whitley Strieber
(Author, Communion)

I have hundreds of favorite words. Funny words like "groak" and "uloid" are delicious to say. Complicated ones, such as "hepaticocholangiocholecystenterostomy," captivate me. I love learning to pronounce them with sufficient facility to include them in ordinary discourse. Words of power draw me. And there are such words, such as "unseen," which have great power. The unseen. He is among the unseen. Unseen, she slipped the phial from her bodice. The only explanation left was this: the unseen. And then there are puns and plays on words, usually considered altogether unseemly, but fun all the same.

Gay Talese
(Author, Thy Neighbor's Wife;
The Kingdom & the Power)

"Effulgent."
    Picked it up as a high school kid reading F. Scott Fitzgerald.

Maria Tallchief
(Prima ballerina)

My mother was a lady of great "courage" and "perseverance." My father had a wonderful sense of "humor" (as did my grandmother Tallchief).

I also like the words "grace" and "elegance."

Amy Tan
(Author, The Joy Luck Club;
The Kitchen God's Wife)

Here's my contribution to your book:

Ing-gai (ing-gi), auxiliary verb, Mandarin Chinese. (1) should have; (2) when coupled with English, used to express a condition of maternal regret: *Ing-gai* never come to United States to raise children who fight against me all the time; (3) must; ought; when coupled with English, used to indicate a filial form of duty: *In-gai* visit Mom this weekend or else we're in big trouble; (4) *"ing-gai* shopping"—the neurotic habit of continuing to look at real estate or the latest computer equipment with the express purpose of torturing yourself with the fact that you spent way too much on last year's purchase.

Etymology. In-gai has been used extensively in

189

Mandarin for thousands of years, but its first appearance in English usage can be traced to a living room in Oakland, California, in 1958, when a Chinese mother was heard to say to her six-year-old American-born daughter, "Turn off TV, *in-gai* practice piano." It was popularized by a small group of San Franciscans in 1983 when the same mother was heard to order chicken in a restaurant while everyone else had ordered fish. When the chicken arrived, the mother eyed it suspiciously, looked enviously at the fish on other people's plates, then sighed and remarked, *"Tʃt! Ing-gai* order fish." Since then the expression *"ing-gai* order fish" has become a useful way to express small regrets over hasty decisions.

Usage. Today *ing-gai* coupled with English continues to be used in all kinds of lamentable situations. Curiously, when used frequently, it has the power to reduce regret to laughter.

Lionel Tiger
(Anthropologist)

Some of my favorite words served as doodles at an academic meeting at the Stanford Law School.

Badminton	Vast	Violin	Happening
Posh	Tiptop	Peanut	Pituitary
Tub	Flounder	Herringbone	Whitewash
Replacement	Harsh	Wringer	Venture
Notice	Pillule	Pendulum	Picturesque
Nomenclature	Knob	Palliative	Pastor
Tremendous	Pernicious	Horseradish	Table
Penumbra	Puerile	Pantaloon	Kerchief
Posh	Happenstance	Effervescent	Endure
Peroration	Wholesome	Punishment	Hillock
Hiss	Pin	Iberia	Siberia
Folderol	Pond	Holbein	Vim 'n'
Hullabaloo	Tally	Handicap	Vigor
Verisimilitude	Portia	Humility	Voracious
Hollywood	Albertina	Hopscotch	
Hey!			

Barbara Tober

(Editor in chief, Bride's *and* Your New Home)

"Metamorphosis." I was born before DDT, and as a child I collected butterflies and moths. At that time the lepidopteran adventures of Edwin Way Teale and Fabré far outshone anything that Gulliver or the Green Hornet could have delivered; besides, one could look up each specimen in the *Encyclopedia of Insects* and imagine traveling from Madagascar to the Amazon, capturing these exquisite creatures, cataloging them, perhaps discovering a new species or genus. It was heady stuff, and to prepare myself for much longer voyages in the future, I made daily and weekly "rounds" to all my mother's gardens, the fields, swamps, and forests, watching the various stages, or "metamorphosis" of the objects of my passion.

This mystical "happening" began every spring with egg cases peppering the back of leaves. These hatched into caterpillars, tiny and swarming at first, growing to an efficient leaf-eating machine covered with spines and horns that made a disgusting mouthful for any bird. Then came the chrysalis (butterfly) or cocoon (moth) nestled in protective leaves or hanging from a branch or plant. And finally, the moment of emergence. The pulsing and straining, as the adult creature struggled to spread its wings and

1.

2.

3.

fly, was breathtaking drama. How could anything so ugly have "metamorphosed" into something so beautiful? It wasn't *birth*. It was, however, a spiritual, if pantheistic, experience.

The classic dictionary definition imbues "metamorphosis" with a sense of witchcraft. But the image of those limp wings, hardening into gaudy kites, conjures up bravado rather than sorcery. We have all felt ugly, unworthy, and dispirited. But as we face the morning mirror each day, and prepare to push on, this mystical "happening"—this metamorphosis—is the creation of those habits of happiness and optimism that conquer our fears. Daily life will always challenge us; our only guarantee is the courage to emerge.

Diana Townsend-Butterworth
(Educator, author, Your Child's First School)

When my son said his first words, I began to suspect a familiar genetic predisposition to philology. We had been eagerly awaiting the expected "Ma Ma" or "Da Da." Instead what we heard was "Badenbaden." A few years later my five-month-old daughter proudly pronounced her first words: "potato" and "porridge," rolling her tongue over the syllables with obvious relish. This was clearly a piece of linguistic bravado since we knew she hated both potatoes and porridge with a passion.

I decided to query my mother about my own early linguistic development and found that I had started out in a normal enough fashion with the usual assortment of common nouns and action verbs. But a few years later I was heard muttering Heffalump, broccoli, Jaberwocky, Rumpelstiltskin, and Czechoslovakia to myself as I drifted off to sleep.

My mother became concerned when she caught me reading the dictionary at dinner one night. She rushed me off to the pediatrician, who immediately made the diagnosis "philology in situ." He assured her that the disorder, although usually incurable, was rarely fatal, and there were few disabling side effects aside from the desire to spend an abnormal amount of time browsing through the stacks of libraries and a predilection for the company of other philologists.

During my adolescent years I turned to writing, relishing the sound of words such as "ecstasy," "aesthetic," "sublime," and "serendipitous."

By the time I got to Harvard, I found that philology had reached epidemic proportions — I was suddenly awash in a sea of Gregorian chants, Spenserian symbolism, and metaphysical dilemmas. After graduation, there was a brief interlude of Tiffany table settings, Baccarat crystal, Castilian mantillas, and marquise diamonds.

In graduate school linguistic analysis, multivariate statistical techniques, undifferentiated psychological syndromes, epidemiological studies, and sushi bars claimed my attention. But a few years later as a new mother I found McDonald's, Snuglis, Dr. Denton's, and Pampers cropping up in conversation with increasing frequency and I often fell asleep meditating on the zen of maternity leave, nannies, and Teuschers.

Fuddruckers, homework, glass ceilings, Nintendo, and vegetarian pizza came next. But now that my first book is in the hands of the gods and the book buyers, and my children have reached the age of responsibility, thirteen and eleven respectively, I'm back to simple, concrete, everyday nouns such as "agent," "advance," "editor," and "royalties," though I occasionally catch myself muttering to my computer about "existentialism," "backlash," and "metacognition."

Joseph F. Traub

(Edwin Howard Armstrong Professor of Computer Science, Columbia University)

Here's my favorite word:

"Information." In 1959, as a new Ph.D., my intuition told me that *information* was central to solving certain kinds of scientific problems over a broad spectrum of fields. I began what would be a thirty-five-year research focus on the relationship between information, uncertainty, and complexity, which has eventually evolved into a field in its own right, known as *information-based complexity,* a field that is internationally studied, with its own research journal, and with regular international symposia and workshops.

Roughly speaking, the aim of information-based complexity is to tease out the *laws of information,* just as physicists have discovered the laws of matter and energy. (This is distinct from *information theory,* a phrase coined by Claude Shannon. In a conversation I once had with Shannon, he readily agreed that his celebrated work was a mathematical theory of communication, not information.)

We know that in the real world, information is usually partial or incomplete; contaminated by error; and has costs attached. Knowing that, can we deal optimally with uncertainty? I believe we can. Laws about information would lead to eco-

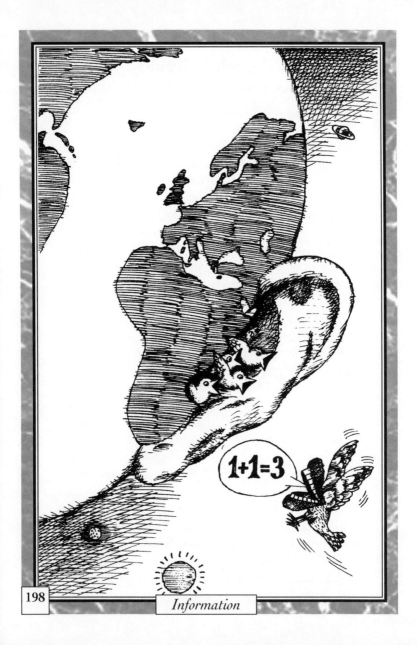

Information

nomical solutions when information is scarce and very costly. In addition, laws would facilitate effective resolution of situations where we are inundated by staggering amounts of information that must be scanned with the hope of drawing the best inferences.

I have speculated that laws of information might even lead to problems in science that we could say with assurance were unsolvable, questions whose answers were—no matter how clever we are—forever unknowable.

Laurence Tribe
(Professor of Law, Harvard Law School)

Favorite word: "whisper."

Desmond M. Tutu
(Anglican Archbishop of Cape Town, Nobel Peace Prize recipient)

Words that I like are "tremendous" and "wonderful." They roll out so wonderfully.

John Updike

(Author, Rabbit Redux; Couples; Odd Jobs)

When I was a young writer in my twenties, I was told that I overused the word "lambent." Recently at the age of sixty, I received word (sic) that the word "conjuration" appeared three times toward the end of a collection of essays, *Odd Jobs.* I am aware in myself of a fondness for "anfractuous" and "phosphorescent," possibly because that is how the world seems to me.

Sander Vanocur

(Television commentator and personality)

After shuttling between Nantucket and Santa Barbara for the past fifteen years, I have concluded that my favorite words are: "capital," "trust fund," and "probate."

Gwen Verdon

(Actress, dancer, Damn Yankees; Sweet Charity)

Beloved
Providence
Junie Moon—My Cat
Morning
Farewell

Patricia Volk
(Author, All It Takes)

I've always been partial to *fuh-∂rayt, fuh-∫him-mele∂, fuh-cocktuh, fuh-blon∂jet,* and *fuh-tu∫hte∂.* I was even thinking of starting a singing group called The Five Fuhs. These words are all different but interchangeable. They mean crazy, mixed up, addled, lost, and wiped out. Just saying them and shrugging makes you feel better. I also love the Italian word for raincoat, *impermeabile,* because saying it is like being in an opera. And in high school biology, I fell in love with "euglena." I use "euglena" every chance I get, as in "It's raining today. I wonder if that's good for the euglenas." "Euglena" is the best word. You can't say it without smiling.

Just for the record, my least favorite word is "dearth." I can never remember what it means because it sounds like the opposite.

Tom Wallace

(Literary agent, The Wallace Agency)

My favorite words? Can anyone who is at all conscious of words and is at the same time halfway articulate have favorites? I guess mine, if they are really favorites at all, have to do with various stages of my life. Prep school: "shoe." Anything admirable, as in "white shoe." College and graduate school: "etiolated." When it comes from Bill Buckley's carefully pursed lips, it sounds truly "euphonious." Publishing: a "popcorn read." A sales manager at a publishing house at which I once worked so characterized any books with legs, a book which ran out of the bookstores, i.e., a book whether fiction or nonfiction, serious or frivolous, which was a "page-turner." Literary agent: Can there be any word with the authority and clarity of "commission"? As in 10 percent or 15 percent. Obviously this does not refer to military rank, presidential panels, or professional baseball, basketball, and hockey potentates. Finally: The word that has meant the most to me in my many years as a student, reader, editor, and agent is "booklover." Someone who can get the same kick from a 5×8, $6 \ 1/8 \times 9 \ 1/4$, paperback or hardcover volume, sewn or perfect bound, that others get from the Sunday *New York Times,* a bottle of champagne, or an extra-inning baseball game.

Wendy Wasserstein
(Playwright, The Heidi Chronicles)

"Beguiling" is a favorite word of mine. Better than charming, with a little mischief thrown in. On a directive—Girls Be Guiling. I want to learn.

"Coney Island," because I have no idea why "island" is pronounced "eyeland." Shouldn't that be the Pearle Vision Center and not a spot of land amidst the water? But I suppose it's better than being an "isthmus," which sounds like a decongestant on holiday.

Nancy Willard
(Poet, novelist, Water Walker; Sister Water)
The Pamplemousse Observed

Pamplemousse—a word, I thought, straight out of Edward Lear, and without knowing what it meant, I fell in love with the word during a dictation in a high school French class: *Le pamplemousse atteint la grosseur d'un melon.*

To a friend who has never studied French, I said: What do you think a *pamplemousse* is?

Beguiling

It's a pampered moose that lives in Argentina, he replied.

It's the French word for "grapefruit," I told him.

But I go on thinking about that moose in Argentina and the earnest young couple who have moved to the pampas to study and tame it. Every night they leave it an offering of the food it loves best. Every night they call,

"Pamplemousse! Pamplemousse!"

They do not know with what sound the *pamplemousse* will answer.

Edward O. Wilson

(Zoologist, two-time winner of the Pulitzer Prize, author, The Ants: The Diversity of Life*)*

"Abyssal." It implies the deep, the dark, and the unknown of the planet's surface.

Gahan Wilson

(Cartoonist, The New Yorker; Playboy)

The best and most resounding personal favorite word I ever heard was Edgar Poe's "cellar door," and I certainly hope you feature it prominently in your book.

I never noticed it until you asked me, but I don't really have an *objet d'art* kind of favorite word, the kind you keep in a niche and admire. My favorite words all seem to be functional.

For example: I can always depend on "pumpkin" to cheer me up.

"Ineffable" helps me increase awareness in the presence of something deserving a good deal more than ordinary attention.

"Good" is the real workhorse. It brings nice things closer every time. You can't beat it for inner glows.

Enclosed find the signed contract. "Contract"* is a word I don't much like, come to think of it.

---

*As a term of the said contract, let the party of the first part (the above-mentioned Frumkes) understand that the words of Wilson (henceforward to be referred to as "the contributor") must be labeled "functional" and their purpose clearly given, or the contributor's choices will make no sense soever. Oyez, oyez.

Hilma Wolitzer

(Author, Tunnel of Love, Silver)

Favorite Words: "morosely" and "wistful."

One of the first books I read on my own as a child was *Penrod* by Booth Tarkington. It opens: "Penrod sat morosely upon the back fence and gazed with envy at Duke, his wistful dog." I didn't know precisely what "morosely" or "wistful" meant, but I felt the *mood* of that sentence and I think I fell in love then with the mystery of language.

Stephen Wright

(Author, The Adventures of Sandy West,
Private Eye)

I'm afraid I have no special words for your book but would note that the entire English language constitutes my favorite words.

I prefer simple words in writing and good colloquial usage, like Somerset Maugham used. And whenever possible, I seek the exact word for any piece of writing I am doing.

My favorite words are those that are found in any collection of my own favorite writers (Maugham, Whitman, the poet Wordsworth, and

Oscar Wilde). Among mystery writers, I prefer Dashiell Hammett and James M. Cain. So, my favorite words are those my favorite writers have penned.

Michael Yogman

(Developmental pediatrician, researcher, Department of Pediatrics, Harvard Medical School)

My favorite word is "Daddy," "Dada," or just "Da," depending on the age of the person saying it. The word has special significance for me as a practicing developmental pediatrician, as a researcher studying father-infant play, and of course as the father of two young daughters.

The sound "Da" is important to pediatricians since it is usually one of the first vowel-consonant combinations uttered by the human infant (around six months). As such, it is a developmental landmark indicating the transition from cry and coo vocalizations to babbling and the first real word, signifying the beginnings of language and the intactness of hearing. While the infant initially uses the sound to convey multiple meanings, altering vocal intonations and combining them with pointing gestures, by a year of age it is used more specifically to refer to the father.

209

Although fathers are delighted to hear this word and it can enhance their view of the baby as a socially communicative person, mothers often need reassurance that "Da" is merely an easier consonant to vocalize than "Ma."

When my own daughters first said "Dada," I had the same overpowering emotional response of any new father—i.e., "She really knows me now!"

William Zinsser

(Author, On Writing Well; Writing to Learn)

I don't have a collection of favorite words like "williwaw" that I keep in a display case to moon over. Such words delight me with their music when I see (and hear) them, but unless they fill a precise need—"filigree," "lapidary," "oscillate"—I shy away from using them, wary of being sucked into the bog of pomposity where academic monsters like "adumbrate" and "ineluctable" lurk. My favorite words, which I spend a lot of time rummaging for, are hundreds of simple, vivid replacements for words that are just too dull to give writing a sense of freshness. "Brazen," for example. Used instead of "bold," not only does it take the reader by surprise with its piquant *z,* but its sound perfectly conveys its meaning. A brazen scheme is more than merely bold; listen and you'll probably hear a mountebank. I write by ear, and sound is usually what leads me to what I'm groping for. I still remember the pleasure of finding exactly the word I needed to catch what had exhilarated me as a young GI riding a train across North Africa during World War II, getting my first exposure to the Arab world. It was the Arab hubbub at the stations.

Elmo R. Zumwalt, Jr.
(Admiral, U.S. Navy [Ret.])

My favorite word is "retromingent."

I thought it was particularly intriguing when Ben Bradlee, then editor of *The Washington Post,* reportedly used it in describing Reed Irvine of Accuracy in Media.

My second most popular word is "supercalifragilisticexpealidotious," which I enjoy using frequently with my grandchildren.